Essential Youth

Why your church needs young people

ANDY HICKFORD

Authentic
LIFESTYLE

First published in 1988 by Kingsway Publications
This edition published in 2003 by Spring Harvest Publishing
Division and Authentic Lifestyle

09 08 07 06 05 04 03   7 6 5 4 3 2 1

Authentic Lifestyle is an imprint of Authentic Media,
PO Box 300, Kingstown Broadway, Carlisle, Cumbria CA3 0QS, UK
and
Box 1047, Waynesboro, GA 30830-2047, USA
www.paternoster-publishing.com

British Library Cataloguing in Publication Data

A catalogue record for this book is available from the British Library

ISBN 1-85078-542-2

Print Management by Adare Carwin
Printed and Bound in Denmark by Nørhaven Paperback

About the Author

Andy Hickford is the minister of Maybridge Community Church in Worthing, West Sussex. For ten years he was a youth minister at Stopsley Baptist Church in Luton. A popular speaker and writer, he is married to Cerys and they have three children.

Contents

Section Three: Essential Youth

Preface to the second edition

My special thanks to Jonathan Chilvers for his invaluable work in helping me prepare this second edition. Since I originally sat down to write *Essential Youth* in 1995-6, cultural change has hurried on apace both within and beyond the church and without his help in reflecting some of these changes this reprint would have felt seriously dated.

Having said that, it's nearly eight years since I was last employed as a youth worker so what on earth am I doing allowing a book to be republished that's based on experiences of nearly a decade ago?

After all, the teenagers I wrote about in the first edition are now among the youth leaders who might read this second edition. Firstly, I believe that many of the principles I explore, especially those learned from missionaries about culture and cross-cultural evangelism, remain of vital importance to the whole church today.

Secondly, my subsequent years of wider church leadership have reinforced those early lessons as a youth worker in Luton. In fact, many of the things in the first edition I now believe even more strongly than I did then.

Thirdly, the transition from a 'modern' to 'postmodern' society is neither sudden nor clear cut. Developing an awareness of this underlying cultural shift is just as important today as it was six years ago.

Finally, the majority of churches in this country remain

in a sorry state and I still passionately believe that by working with young people God graciously provides us with some significant keys to unlock the way forward.

My prayer is that this second edition will continue to resource all those on that journey.

ANDY HICKFORD
AUGUST 2003

Introduction

I first met James when he was twelve years old. I noticed him because it was snowing and he was standing outside the local Co-op in only a tee-shirt. He was frozen. We got chatting and I gave him a lift home. That was the start of a friendship which was to last more than ten years.

Of all the young people I have ever worked with, James has made me struggle the most with what it means to share Jesus with someone of a different background. For without doubt, though he only lived down the street from me, James and I came from different worlds. His dad was long-term unemployed and bordering on alcoholic. His mum was an acute agoraphobic who rarely left her living room. His older brother was in care and his two younger brothers were already in trouble with the police. His whole outlook on life was entirely different from mine.

He came round one Friday night more excited than I had ever seen him. 'Look what I've found,' he said. In his hand was a small wage packet that he had picked up outside a building site on his way home from school. I counted the money. There was £180. I took a deep breath and as gently as possible I said: 'James, you know what I think you should do with this money, don't you?'

His expression changed, he looked me straight in the eye and said quietly: 'And if you were a kid like me, you know what you'd do, don't you?'

I must admit, I had nothing else to say. James never did get the money though. His dad took it off him that night and spent the whole lot in one trip to the off-licence.

With those words though, James had unwittingly focused my task as a Christian youth worker. 'If you were a kid like me …' It was exactly what I needed to do – start thinking like James did, see the world through his eyes, put myself in his position, and begin to try to feel how he must feel. If I were a kid like James, what would doing well at school mean? If I were a kid like James, what would honouring my parents mean? If I were a kid like James, what would fulfilling my potential mean? And supremely, what would it mean to follow Jesus?

Without fully appreciating what was happening, I had started along the road of trying to place the gospel in the context of the people I was working with. In reality, I was setting off in hot pursuit along a track well worn by many a missionary before me.

Little did I know that over the next ten years James was to going teach me more than I was able to teach him. While I tried to help him understand the gospel, James helped me to understand it in ways I had never seen before. While I was trying to help James overcome his background, he helped me overcome mine. While I was trying to help James relate to church, he helped me to see the role of the church more clearly than I had ever seen it before. While I prayed for James to experience Jesus, through working with James I began to understand more of how Jesus wanted to work in my own life.

Evangelism to others also became a process of God's revelation to me. Meeting with James and kids like him was to change my understanding of Christian ministry.

To read this book, then, is to join that same journey of discovery that working with young people can provide. *Essential Youth* is all about how the church can learn about itself and the nature of the gospel in today's world by working with and listening to teenagers.

It's about the problems we face as a church and how working with young people can help solve them.

Essential Youth is organised in three sections, but only the last section deals with some of the specific lessons we can learn. Why? Because to get to that point we must first do our biblical thinking. In times of change it is more important than ever to keep coming back to the Bible for the principles of what we should be doing. After all, we can only learn from young people if they reveal God's truth to us.

Section One is therefore all about culture and the vital role it plays in how we understand the Christian message and live out the Christian faith. Here we see that today's church does not recognise the influence of culture and that we can only begin to see our immediate world more as God would have us see it, with the help of people from different cultures and backgrounds from our own.

Section Two looks at whether young people today can really be said to be people of a different culture. At first it sounds a bit over the top; after all, they live in the same street and speak the same language as we do. However, it's an important section for this reason: if it is valid to see them as a separate cultural group, then it is also valid that God can use them to show us things about our churches that we fail to see at the moment.

Finally, we get to Section Three and the lessons we can learn. Today's church is really struggling with contemporary culture, yet it has in its midst people who belong to that culture and who can be employed in helping the church engage with that culture. These people are the youth of our churches. The world needs them. The church needs them. And for everybody's sake, we need them now.

SECTION ONE

Cultural Captives

Youth work is essential to the church because it forces us to take seriously the issue of culture.

1

Why Do We Do That?
(Culture defined)

I'm confused! When I was young, tattoos were the exclusive domain of hairy bikers and rugged sailors! But now it seems they have become a hot fashion accessory. Young and beautiful women want a tattoo. What is going on?

Think about your haircut and why you have it the way you do. Ask yourself why you bought the clothes that you are wearing right now. Think about the music you listen to or what you ate for your last meal. Think about where you want to go on holiday next year, or whether you like tattoos or not. Think about any of these issues and you start thinking about culture.

Culture is experienced more readily than it can be described. It is the air we breathe. It is the water we swim in. It is everything about our background and environment that shapes the people we are.

So, for example, you are not the first person to have your hair that way or to dress as you do. In making those choices you were first influenced by the styles and fashions around you. You may not view yourself as a fashion victim, but the truth is that you only had a number of options and they were shaped by the culture of which you are part. What does a man wear in the West other than trousers?

It is not as though BHS is doing a special promotion this year on loincloths, is it? However outrageous the colour and cut you choose, when all is said and done they are all still trousers!

THIS YEAR BHS IS NOT DOING A
SPECIAL PROMOTION IN LOINCLOTHS...

The same is true for women. The very fact that women can choose to wear trousers if they want to, let alone have a tattoo, is in itself a cultural statement. In many countries, women do not have the choice. You may not be a fashion victim, but we are all cultural creations.

> 'Culture is an integrated system of beliefs, values, customs and institutions which bind a society together and give it a sense of identity, dignity, security and continuity.'[1]

Shaped and changed by things like our history, technology, language, institutions, art and national identity, culture comes to define our ideas about what is right and wrong, good and bad, our tastes and preferences and our expectations about how we should behave.

In the Philippines it is perfectly normal to go up to your friend and say, 'You're looking fat today,' whereas if I said that to a pal in the supermarket tomorrow I might well get a slap. It would be offensive, because as Brits we tend to avoid honesty in the name of 'getting along', pride ourselves on being tactful and are obsessive about our weight. Yet we rarely stop and question the assumptions that govern our everyday conversations and thoughts.

So, then, culture is the context in which we live our daily lives. In short, 'It's the way we do things round here!'[2]

Cultural specs

Culture's influence is like wearing a pair of glasses. Without our realising it culture has issued us with spectacles through which we see and understand the world. Other writers have called these specs our worldview.

Mike Starkey put it like this: 'My worldview is the pair of mental spectacles through which I view everything, it is the unifying vision which not only affects how I see the world, it even affects what I see there, highlighting some things and masking others, revealing some things as desirable, others to be avoided. ... We all wear a pair of worldview spectacles (whether we know it or not), and none of us could operate without them.'[3]

Invisible power

Culture exerts massive influence on every individual human being through these specs. In many ways, culture defines what we think of as acceptable and even possible.

Seeing the specs

My worst fears were realised the day I tentatively opened the fridge door and, much to the amusement of my undergraduate friends, found that the entire contents of my underwear drawer had become a solid block of ice in the freezer compartment. I was wondering what I was going to do while my Y-fronts defrosted, when one of the African students strode in. He very angrily seized all his food from the fridge and threw it in the bin. Then he demanded compensation from my friends for making his lunch 'unclean'.

A little put out, I quickly assured him that my pants had only just been washed, but it was no good. I was obviously missing the point entirely. This was a cultural thing. He could not 'hear' my explanations about student humour. Underwear and food were kept separate where he came from, and he wanted his money back. In the circumstances I thought it only fair to try to make sure that my friends paid up.

Culture can only exercise this kind of power because it goes unnoticed. It is powerful because it is invisible.

It is the very normality of everything around us that seduces us into believing that culture does not affect us too much. In reality, entirely the opposite is true.

George Gerbner put it like this: 'What people learn best is not what their teachers teach, or what their parents preach, but what their cultures in fact cultivate.'[4]

Cultural essentials

For the Christian, discovering these cultural specs is very important. It helps us to understand the way we think and behave, it helps us recognise the pressures we live under, and most importantly it helps clear away those areas of our life that Jesus wants to change.

Don't become so well-adjusted to your culture that you fit into it without even thinking. Instead, fix your attention on God (Rom. 12:2, The Message).[5]

True conversion to Christ is bound, therefore, to strike at the heart of our cultural inheritance. Jesus Christ insists on dislodging from the centre of our world whatever idol previously reigned there and occupying the throne himself.[6]

That is not to say that all of our own culture's influence is bad – some of it is extremely good. The point is, as Christians we need to recognise its influence in the first place.

Sadly, however, for the majority of Christians the issue of culture remains largely hidden and the glasses undiscovered.

To sum up so far: culture's influence in shaping the way we think and behave is enormous and at the same time profoundly unnoticeable.

NOTES

1. *The Willowbank Report* (Lausanne Commission for World
   Evangelization, 1978), p.7. For futher definitions of culture see Paul
   G. Hiebert, *Anthropological Insights for Missionaries* (Baker Books, 1985)
   p.30ff
2. Roy McCloughry, *Tomorrow's World* (Christian Institute Lectures,
   1996).
3. Mike Starkey, *Fashion and Style* (Monarch, 1995), pp.23–24
4. George Gerbner quoted in Reynolds R. Ekstrom, *Pop Culture* (Don
   Bosco Multimedia, 1989), p.32
5. E. Peterson, *The Message* (Navpress, 1993), p.386
6. *The Willowbank Report* (LCWE), p.20

2

Trapped
(The church's problem with culture)

Introduction

Culture's power to influence our lives without us realising it has big consequences for the church. On the one hand, our discipleship often fails to break out of the world into God's church. On the other, our evangelism struggles to break free from the church's own culture in order to reach the world. It sounds absurd, but the church today is largely a cultural captive.

I am suggesting in this book that by making work with young people a priority we shall discover, almost by accident, the keys to unlock this situation. But first, let's look in more detail at the nature of the captivity.

Cultural discipleship

> The first call of the gospel of Christ is not to proclamation ... nor is it social action. The first call of the gospel of Christ is incarnation – living out something that is radically different.[1]

Discipleship is following Jesus. It is the process by which we become more like Christ. It is about learning to see the world as God sees it, developing biblical thinking, and starting to relate to people and our environment as Jesus would. To be a disciple is to be a pilgrim – journeying through this world, living in anticipation of the next, bringing the future into the present, dancing to a different rhythm, and marching to a different drum beat from the world.

The great danger on this journey is being insufficiently aware of our own cultural specs, confusing our culture's values with what we think are Christian values. Even one of the great evangelists, D.L. Moody, made the mistake of labelling the four great sins of his day as the 'theatre, Sunday newspapers, evolution and a disregard for the Sabbath'.[2] One can't help thinking he missed a few! Moody had allowed his cultural specs to colour his understanding of true discipleship.

Our cultural blindness often still goes right to the heart of what it means to be a Christian. In recent years we've begun to see several areas in which the Western imitation of Christ is clearly compromised by our culture.

Rational faith

Rationalism in its proper sense 'is perhaps best defined as the doctrine that the external world can be known by reason and reason alone.'[3] It's the idea that the only things worth knowing are things we can prove and understand, and it was a central tenet of modernism. Developing in the mid-eighteenth century, when Descartes proclaimed 'I think, therefore I am,' it said universal human reason and logic would provide the solutions to all of humanity's problems. Progress was defined as logical and scientific advancement, meaning that cultures both within and beyond the West that didn't employ rationalism as their foundation were seen as 'uncivilised'. With human reason as its idol, rationalism was one of the foundational pillars of the modern Western world.

Christians growing up in this environment very readily picked up on a strand of the Bible's teaching about loving God with our minds (Mt. 22:37), thinking with renewed minds (Rom. 12:2), and setting our minds on things above (Col. 3:2) – not just because it was biblical, but because it was part of modern Western culture. It led to great advances in Christian scholarship that have been of tremendous value to the church, but for some people loving God with our minds became limiting him with our minds. What they could not fully understand and find a proof text for was either ignored or dismissed as unbiblical.[4]

Ironically, when the world began to move on from some of the extreme cultural values of rationalism and modernism the church clung to them as sacrosanct. Christianity was, and largely remains, trapped in rational culture.

Feeling faith

Rationalism became so claustrophobic it provoked a huge reaction in the Western world that began with the Romantic poets in the Victorian era, when rationalism was at its height. Faith in human reason was broken down by the horrors of World War I and the cold 'rationality' of the Holocaust. By the 1970s this had produced what has become known as postmodernity:

> 'Postmodernism is a reaction against modernism, which had reason with a capital R.'[5]

'Postmodernism refers to an intellectual mood and an array of cultural expressions that call into question the ideals, principles and values that lay at the heart of the modern mind-set. Postmodernity, in turn, refers to an emerging epoch, the era in which we are living , the time when the postmodern outlook increasingly shapes our society.'[6]

The postmodern world is a world which understands itself through biological rather than mechanistic models; a world where people see themselves as belonging to the environment rather than over it or apart from it. A world distrustful of institutions, hierarchies, centralised bureaucracies and male dominated organisations. It is a world in which networks and local grass root activities take precedence over large scale structures and grand designs; a world in which the book age is giving way to the screen age; a world hungry for spirituality yet dismissive of systematised religion. It is a world in which image and reality are so deeply intertwined that it is difficult to draw the line between the two.[7]

Intellectuals began to question whether discovering knowledge was actually a good thing any more. (How could it be when the latest technologies had been so horribly abused in two world wars?) They became increasingly sceptical about complete belief systems and philosophies. (Had they not been seen to be thinly veiled bids for power and coercion?) In this new world there emerged more ways of knowing than merely intellectual. More ways of being than simply the rational.

Once again the church mirrored this cultural shift. Christians growing up in these generations have less of a problem accepting a supernatural God who is to be experienced and whose infinite ways and thoughts are beyond our finite understanding (Is. 55:8; 1 Cor. 2:9–10). Once again, though, there was an over-reaction. As a teenager in the heady days of charismatic renewal in the 1970s, I was told on many occasions, 'Don't think – feel!' No longer was rational thought the foundation of faith – experience was.

Both rational and feeling faith have cut and pasted the Bible. God's word holds the two in perfect tension. He is to be worshipped and known in both thought and experience (1 Cor. 14:15–20). Nevertheless, both forms of culturally compromised Christianity are alive and depressingly well within evangelicalism today.

'Beware of cultural captivity. Study today's philosophy and tomorrow's theology will come as no surprise. The former queen of the sciences has lost her throne and is now working as a fashion model.'[8]

Private faith

Another cultural pressure that imperceptibly pushed Christianity in an unbiblical direction was the privatising of faith. As society became multicultural, a way of living together evolved that avoids constant arguing about religion. Over time, there emerged in our culture a distinction between the private and public worlds of faith. Religious faith became respected and valued when practised by individuals, but unwelcome and opposed if that private faith 'strayed' into the public domain with implications for others.

Christians brought up in this culture were able to see the strand of biblical teaching that emphasised the devotional aspects of discipleship – such as worship, prayer and Bible study – and got into them in a big way, spawning in the process a whole industry of conferences, books and resources. But the truth is that they did so not just because the Bible says they are important, but because the culture said it was OK. If push came to shove, these generations of Christians might indulge in the occasional time of personal evangelism, but to suggest, for example, that to be salt and light in our world means Christians should be politically active is entirely alien to their thinking.

Private faith has also meant that Christian teaching on holiness has tended to be preoccupied with our 'private' lives:

> By focussing their attention on gambling or drink, [Christians] ignore the way in which they have unconsciously absorbed their neighbours' views on virtually everything else. They strain at a gnat and swallow a whole cultural camel.[9]

... STRAIN AT A GNAT AND SWALLOW A WHOLE CULTURAL CAMEL.

So today the public world is a world of 'facts', a world dominated by politics and business. It is an aggressive, critical world; an environment in which there are many who would seek to oppose and discredit Christianity, as well as offer alternatives.

The private world is a world of values, a world of no rights and no wrongs, a world which is cosy and safe and where respect for personal choice reigns.

At the start of the twenty-first century, evangelicalism often retreats on this point and is only just beginning to realise that we must break out. It is strange when you think about it. The Romans persecuted Christians precisely because they refused to retreat to the private world. They believed that if Christ was truth, he was truth for the whole empire. How times change.

As with animals, so for the church. The price of conservation is captivity.[10]

> 'What once turned the world upside down
> has now turned in on itself.'[11]

Material faith

Storing up for ourselves 'treasures on earth' is hardly a
new issue. Even in the third century Cyprian was stark ·
about this area of cultural captivity for Christians: 'Their
property held them in chains, chains which shackled their
courage and choked their faith, hampered their judgment
and throttled their souls.'[12]

This same cultural entrapment continues, however.
Our calling to 'simplicity, generosity, and contentment'
as John Stott[13] has put it seems to be comprehended only
by a minority. We still assume that as we get older and
progress, we will try and buy bigger houses, better cars,
have more holidays and acquire all the necessary acces-
sories for a comfortable lifestyle.

Deep down we are at least intellectually aware that in
a world of limited resources this means that the poor will
always stay poor, our environment will degenerate and
that such ambition is culturally not biblically driven. Our
cultural conditioning makes exploring the alternatives
seem so unpalatable and unreasonable, however, that
most never try.

As Tom Sine puts it: 'Many of us have unquestionably
attempted to layer our faith right over the top of the secular
values with which we have been raised. We have simply
accepted cultural expectations (such as looking after
Number One) as largely unquestioned givens.'[14]

We have not recognised the exclusive nature of discipleship. We have taken on cultural baggage and tried to
christianise it. The agenda has been set and we've tried

to add a nice God-type 'any other business' at the end, when all the time Christians should refuse to accept the agenda in the first place. We have tried to see where Jesus may fit into our lifestyle, when actually it is where our lifestyle fits into Jesus that is the real question.

'God wants to start messing around with our cultural values, to transform our life direction from upwardly mobile to outwardly ministering.'[15]

Culture's influence on our attempts to follow Christ is a real problem. The crisis in the church is one of product quality. The question at the heart of discipleship is: Where are we going to get our values from – our culture or Jesus? When our imitation of Christ is compromised by our material, private, rational and feeling faith we are no different from anybody else. The dreadful truth is that we don't really have that much to offer.

'Show the world a real, living, self-sacrificing, toiling, triumphing, hard-working religion and the world will be influenced by it. Anything less than that and they will turn round and spit on it.'[16]

Cultural evangelism – how we have failed to break out of the church

Blindness to our cultural conditioning becomes even more destructive when it comes to evangelism. Nowhere is this more clearly seen than in early foreign mission experience. Well-meaning missionaries, who were largely unaware of how their faith was so tied up in their own culture, often imposed their culture when they introduced their faith. It seems crazy now but they even took out organs and choir robes to people who played the drum and wore loincloths.[17]

Today the same forces of ignorance are at work in evangelism on our doorsteps. We are once again failing to take due consideration of the people we are trying to reach. In our enthusiasm to explain that Jesus is the answer, we overlook the fact that nobody is asking the question. We are occasionally in touch with our culture, but nearly always out of tune with it. As a TV producer told Steve Chalke, 'You evangelicals are always trying to answer question number 17, when we are not even sure what question number 1 is. You need to begin where we are, not where you want us to be. Some of you are worse than politicians. It makes no difference what the question is, you always tell us what you want us to hear anyway.'[18]

...WE OVERLOOK THE FACT THAT NOBODY IS ASKING THE QUESTION

With the vast majority of the country not Christian, we have to ask ourselves whether people consciously reject Christ or whether it is more subtle than that. 'Is it because people were being offered something they did not realise they needed, in a vocabulary that they did not comprehend, by someone who seemed indifferent to the needs they knew they had?'[19]

The problem is more than one of communication. Our cultural entrapment is more serious than that. The real problem in evangelism is that the church is communicating exactly what it is – out of touch. Essentially we can't engage with our world today because the Christian culture we have developed around us alienates the church from normal people. We use different words, listen to different music, go to different places, read different books and even go on different holidays.

In her autobiography, *The Kindness of Strangers*, Kate Adie illustrates this powerfully when she writes about attending the funerals of many of the victims of the tragic fire at Bradford Football Ground in 1985.

'What I was totally unprepared for was church after church into which came noisy schoolchildren shouting What's this then? What's a church? Why should we shush? What happens here? Why can't I sit where I like? Many were dressed in party clothes, all bright shirts and spangles, skimpy satin disco skirts and rude T-shirts. They said their old nans had told told them 'to wear their best' and so here they were in their glad rags. They sat through the service in blank amazement, as if attending a tribal ritual in a far off country – which in effect they were. They squirmed and chatted. The religious background which I've had many an occasion to question was unknown to them and so traditional funerals were inexplicable.'[20]

So strong is this entrapment, the writer Peter Wagner

suggests that it takes a convert just five years in a church before he ceases to know any non-Christians.[21]

How badly we need to hear the words of wisdom written many years ago that take the issue of culture in evangelism seriously: 'Conversion involves repentance, but this does not require the convert to step right out of his former culture into a Christian sub-culture which is totally distinctive. Conversion is not migration, it is the personal discovery of the meaning of the universal Christ, within the old framework of race, language and tradition.'[22]

At the end of the day our primary concern must continue to be what God thinks of the church, not what society thinks of it. However, we place so many unnecessary obstacles in the way of people coming to faith that our practice of church urgently needs reviewing. Perhaps the greatest task facing evangelicals at the beginning of the twenty-first century is not so much to build bridges into the community, but rather to make those bridges unnecessary in the first place.

To do so, we will need to get out of the culture trap.

Summary of Chapter 2

Beware, you will need to read this carefully. Here is the ultimate irony. Our culture has too much influence on our Christian discipleship, while at the same time not having enough influence on our church evangelism!

We have become caught between two unpalatable options: to be relevant but indistinctive, or distinctive but irrelevant. Little wonder then that the church has problems with culture.

In the next chapter we shall see that our own cultural entrapment can be both exposed and helped by working with people of a different culture.

Notes

1. Tom Sine, 'The Wrong Dream', *Tear Times*, Autumn 1996, p.15
2. Dave Tomlinson, *The Post-Evangelical* (Triangle Books, 1995), p.41
3. Alister McGrath, *Christian Theology – an Introduction* (Blackwell, 2001) p.89
4. For a detailed treatment of how the Enlightenment affected Christianity see David Bosch, *Transforming Mission* (Orbis, 2001) pp.267-344
5. Phillips and Okholm, *Christian Apologetics in a Post Modern World* (IVP)
6. Stanley Grenz, *A Primer on Postmodernism* p.12 (Eerdmans, 1996)
7. Dave Tomlinson, *The Post-Evangelical* (Triangle Books, 1995), p.75
8. Os Guinness
9. Tony Walter, *A Long Way From Home* (Exeter: Paternoster, 1979)
10. Os Guinness, *The Gravedigger File* (Hodder & Stoughton, 1983), p.74
11. Os Guinness, *The Gravedigger File*, p.91
12. Cyprian, *The Lapsed*, p.11
13. John Stott, *Issues Facing Christians Today* (Marshall Morgan & Scott, 1984), ch.12
14. Tom Sine, *Taking Discipleship Seriously*
15. Tom Sine, 'The Wrong Dream', *Tear Times*, Autumn 1996, p.15
16. Catherine Booth, *Aggressive Christianity* (The Salvation Army S&P Department, re-published 1986), p.9
17. See Paul G. Hiebert, *Anthropological Insights for Missionaries* (Baker, 1985) p.184; Andrew F. Walls, *The Missionary Movement in Christian History* (T&T Clark, 1996) p.93, and for a review of the missionary movements compliance with colonialism in general see David Bosch, *Transforming Mission* (Orbis, 2001) pp.302-313
18. 'Engaging the Culture', *Alpha Magazine*, October 1994
19. Martyn Eden (ed), *Britain on the Brink* (Crossway Books, 1993), p.8
20. Kate Adie, *The Kindness of Strangers* (Headline, 2002) p.215
21. Peter Wagner quoted by Alison Burnett in *Alpha* article on Willow Creek 1993
22. Bishop Kenneth Cragg, *The Call of the Minaret* (Lutterworth, 1956). Quoted by John Stott, *Christian Mission in the Modern World* (Kingsway, 1986), p.123

3

Exposé
(How we are helped by working with different cultures)

> I could not have come to this critical stance in relation to my own culture without the experience of living in another.[1]

Words fail to do justice to my embarrassment. In front of everybody in the room, Jim was holding my hand, earnestly looking me in the eyes and singing to me! I wanted the ground to swallow me up, especially when another of my friends got out a video camera.

This incident makes no sense unless the circumstances are understood. It took place in the slums of Addis Ababa, Ethiopia. It was a classic clash of cultures. I had given Jim (short for Baroojimah) the gift of a hat and as he could not speak any English he communicated his gratitude in a way that was entirely in keeping with his culture – he sang to me. I was the only one in the whole room who appeared in any way uncomfortable. Everything about my background said that grown men did not sit next to each other holding hands, looking into each other's eyes and singing! It did not make what Baroojimah did wrong, of course. It was just that the cultures he and I had grown up in were so vastly different.

Takes one to know one

There is no clearer way of discovering what lenses you have in your cultural spectacles than by having them knocked askew when you bump into another culture. There is nothing like that culture jolt to let you see that you are also a cultural product and your values, tastes and standards have all been shaped by your background as surely as your hosts' have.

This experience can be of even greater significance for the Christian. It is perhaps only in this cross-cultural encounter that we are almost forced to begin the difficult but vital task of evaluating what of our Christian practice is authentically Christian and what is of our society's or our church's culture. In other words, to begin the Romans 12 process of refusing to be squeezed into the world's mould.

Not that a 'freestanding' gospel completely separate from culture ever exists of course. If God had intended that then Jesus would not have been born a Jew. It is precisely because of the incarnation (God became man) that all followers of Christ have had to go through life sifting and sorting the differences between following Jesus and following the ways of the world.

Incident to insight

It was only slowly that I began to see that I too had in a measure co-opted Jesus into the world view of my culture.

It was an incident in an Indian village that made me realise this. I was taking a group of village teachers through Mark's gospel. My Tamil wasn't very good but I was fairly confident of my theology, fresh as I was from theological college. All went well until we reached the first exorcism. Westminster College had taught me very little about casting out demons. My exposition was not very impressive. These village teachers looked at me with growing perplexity, and then one of them said, 'Why are you making such heavy weather of a simple matter?' and proceeded to rattle off half a dozen cases of exorcism in his own congregation in the past few months. Of course, I could have said, 'My dear brother, if you will let me arrange for you to come to Cambridge and take a proper training in modern science and then a postgraduate psychology degree, you will discover that Freud and Jung have explained everything.' In other words, 'If you will permit me to induct you into my culture, you will see things as they really are.' But this was a Bible study and Mark's gospel was open before us, saying precisely what it does. Inwardly, I had to admit that he was much closer to the text than I was. Outwardly, I kept quiet and went on to the next passage.[2]

So many of the great mission writers talk of how these awkward encounters set them off on their path to discovery about the nature of the gospel that it is hard not to conclude that the more difficult the cultural challenge, the greater the resulting insight into the gospel. Vincent Donovan spent twenty years in East Africa:

I can still remember when I first tried to communicate the gospel to a Masai tribesman, sitting under a tree in his red blanket. He had never been more than a few miles from his home. But I could see in my conversation with him that he valued three things: that he could walk fifty miles a day; that he knew all that there was to know about his cows; and that he was a Masai, the most important people on the earth. He could see that I was not a Masai, that I did not know a thing about cows and that I could hardly walk ten miles. So to him I was completely valueless. He had an air of superiority that began to get to me. I asked myself, how can I communicate my very important message when he can't care less about anything I have to offer?[3]

So often as a youth worker I have gone through the same range of emotions and asked myself the same questions. Talking in night clubs to lads whose only interest is women, with boys at the park who just want to play football (and I was always rubbish at football), with a group of travellers' kids who view me with utter bewilderment, with school groups and even kids at church, my question has so often been the same. How can I communicate my very important message when they couldn't care less about anything I have to offer?

Every time, though, I keep coming back to James, the lad I spoke of in my preface. 'If you were a kid like me' keeps going around and around in my head.

One afternoon after school he came round to my flat. He looked so fed up I asked him what was wrong. 'The kids at school are calling me gypo because of my sad clothes,' he said. Now I had read the books on handling personal anger and helping people through rejection, so I said the right thing, 'And how did that make you feel, James?'

'Dunno,' came the reply. 'I just threw a brick at them!'

At this point in our relationship the generational tensions were less than they were to become later. Initially the gap between us had its roots in class, family, education and wealth. At twelve he knew I was not just older – we were different. With hindsight, I see now that even before

I met him, James had lost hope, he knew he was a failure. Life was not about dreams but existence. He was already angry.

As I spent time with James I slowly began to realise how deep the differences between us went. To do well at school for me had meant going to university, for James it meant not getting permanently excluded. To eat well had meant for me having a balanced diet of three square meals a day. For James it meant having some change in his pocket for chips. 'Going home' was for me a safe and peaceful place. For James there was no place of peace in his life. The best bit of Christmas for me was celebrating with all the family. For James it was being allowed to stay in bed all day and watch television.

Eventually it dawned on me: if we were so very different, why was I trying to introduce James to Jesus the same way Jesus had been introduced to me? Why did I expect James to follow Jesus like I did? Nothing else in our lives was the same, so why should Christianity be any different? Of course, the principles would be consistent, but surely I had to expect the practice of faith to be very different?

So I started the process of unravelling my faith as a Christian, asking myself what was essential to be passed on to James and what was simply my culture's practice and therefore inappropriate to James' world. I was discovering what the missionaries had learnt before me. The best way to discover how our culture has unwittingly shaped our Christian faith is to try and pass on that faith to people of a different culture.

Any amount of cross-cultural experience will fail to deliver the church from its culture trap, however, unless it goes hand in hand with a biblical perspective on culture.

NOTES
1. Lesslie Newbigin, *Foolishness to the Greeks* (SPCK, 1985), ch.1
2. Lesslie Newbigin in Jock Stein (ed.), *Mission and the Crisis of Western Culture* (Handel Press, 1989), p.2
3. Thom Hopler, *A World of Difference* (IVP, 1981), p.185

4

Back to the Book
(What the Bible teaches about culture)

Before we look at an overview of what the Bible teaches on culture, a word of warning. As we have already seen, we all come to the Bible biased. 'No one can escape sharing in the mentality and intellectual climate of his own culture.'[1]

Bearing this in mind, we must always be very careful to try not to read into the Bible the prejudices of our own background. Instead, we need to try to interpret the Bible within its original culture and look for principles which still apply to us today.

Culture in the Old Testament

The Old Testament is of limited help when it comes to understanding culture because God had chosen Israel as his special people and God was only to be encountered in and through Israel. There was no good news to share, no commission for the Jews to evangelize other nations.[2] God's intention in electing the Jews was to bless others through them (Gal. 3:8). In practice God's election of the Jews often led to a sense of superiority over other races.

If a Philistine or Midianite decided to become a follower of Yhwh the only way they could do it was to become, to all intents and purposes, a Jew.

This inevitably led to a fairly one-sided presentation of culture in the Old Testament. Israelite culture was the only context in which God could be met so it had to be protected from all other cultures, which in some way might corrupt it.

This theme can be seen from the very first chapter of Genesis when God said: 'Fill the earth and subdue it. Rule over the fish of the sea and the birds of the air and over every living creature.' There seems to be a strong theme in the Old Testament that God's people are not to be helpless victims of their circumstances, but can live according to different priorities.

Noah and his family were saved from the flood precisely because they were not like the rest of society, and God called Abraham to 'Leave your country, your people and your father's household and go to the land I will show you' (Gen. 12:1).

Under the leadership of Moses and Joshua, God's people were wanderers with no fixed home. When they finally entered the promised land, they did so with clear instructions to behave very differently from its previous occupants: 'When you enter the land the Lord your God is giving you, do not learn to imitate the detestable ways of the nations there' (Deut. 18:9). Indeed, they were commanded to remain distant from their neighbours (Ex. 34:15).

Joseph, Daniel and Nehemiah are seen as heroes of the faith, because at no time did they compromise their beliefs under pressure from a foreign culture. This theme is picked up again in the wisdom literature of the Old Testament, where there is often an appeal to the reader not to succumb to being like all the rest (Prov. 7:25–26).

The ministry of the prophets also had this strong counter-culture theme. When Israel conformed to the practices of the surrounding nations, by worshipping idols or looking to other nations instead of God for alliances and support, they were strongly condemned (Amos 3:4; Is. 3:1–2).

Generally speaking, then, the Old Testament seems to have a 'come out and be separate' focus to its teaching on how God's people should relate to the cultures of the world. However, that's not to say that foreign cultures should be understood entirely negatively in the Old Testament.

POLYGAMY WAS TAKEN UP BY THE ISRAELITES...

There are times when God appears more tolerant of Jewish culture being affected by surrounding nations. Polygamy, the practice of taking more than one wife, is a foreign idea taken up by the Israelites and not explicitly condemned in the Old Testament. Even the fundamental concept of covenant had equivalent cultural parallels in other nations.[3] In 1 Kings 8, God even appears to concede to the request to give Israel a king so they could be 'like the other nations' – despite the dire warnings of its cost from the prophet Samuel (1 Sam. 8:19–20).

More positively, during the exile period the prophet Jeremiah actively encouraged Jews living in Babylon to 'seek the peace and prosperity of the city' and to 'pray to the Lord for the welfare of the city' (Jer. 29:7). In other words, to make a positive contribution to the life and culture of Babylon.[4]

The New Testament

In the New Testament, mission changes everything. Now there is a command to share the faith and a God who is no longer tied to one nation but is Lord of all the nations of the earth (Rom. 16:26), who can be known and followed everywhere. Though there remains a strong emphasis on not allowing faith in Jesus to be compromised by the ways of the world (e.g. 1 Jn. 2:15; Rom. 12:1; Col. 3:8–11), the New Testament becomes an exciting story of how Jesus seeks to redeem people of every culture, meeting people in their world but challenging it at the same time.

The Evangelical Fellowship of the Anglican Communion has summed up this tension helpfully: 'All cultures have something God-given in them and have categories in which the gospel can begin to be understood. Yet every culture must be tested by scripture and is under the judgement of God.'

THE MINISTRY OF JESUS

Thom Hopler says 'Jesus crossed the cosmic culture barrier' and in doing so provided us with models for cross-cultural communication. For example, the Jews and

Samaritans were such bitter enemies that Jews would take long detours to avoid even travelling through Samaria. Not so Jesus. He went straight through the country and engaged an obvious outcast of even her own people in conversation (Jn. 4:7). In doing so, Hopler suggests, Jesus provides us with four helpful principles for cross-cultural evangelism:

- honest acknowledgement of our background and how it shapes our beliefs (vv. 9, 19–20)
- overcoming prejudice and difficulty by careful listening (vv. 13–15)
- finding elements of truth in a different culture (v. 17b)
- challenging what is wrong (vv. 22–24).

From the dialogues of Jesus, it is also possible to see how the circumstances of an individual would to some extent at least shape what Jesus said to them. For example, in Luke 10:25–37 and Mark 10:17–25, the lawyer and the rich young ruler ask Jesus the same question yet receive different answers. Jesus appears to be very sensitive to the starting point of his listeners and determined to begin 'where they are'.

Acts

But how would Christianity fare beyond the boundaries of Judaism? It is in the book of Acts that the gospel's interlacing with Greek and Roman culture becomes most intriguing.

'In terms of culture, Paul varied the approach. In Acts 14 in the pagan town of Lystra he spoke very differently to Antioch, which was Jewish (Acts 13) and again to the philosophical Greeks of Ephesus in Acts 19:10. Paul gives two insights: 1) that the cultural background of the recipient must determine what the communicator can present, at least initially. 2) Paul did not change the message, but rearranged the component parts.'[5]

Crossing entrenched cultural barriers with the gospel was a huge challenge, both to individual Christians and the wider church. Peter went through a personal crisis on more than one occasion as God allowed the gospel gradually to dislodge his proud Jewish cultural specs (Acts 10 and 11; Gal. 2:11).

At the Council of Jerusalem in Acts 15, the church faced a huge dilemma. Jewish Christians were trying to establish what of their faith and practice was of the gospel and what was of their culture. What was of the gospel needed to be passed on to the new Gentile churches; what was of their particular Jewish culture did not. The outcome of this defining moment in church history leaves us today with excellent principles for church planting in different cultures:

● give teaching on clear principles (i.e. Acts 15:29)
● give room for on-the-ground interpretation (Acts 15:28)
● send people of faith to model the message (Acts 15:25).

PAUL SWOTS UP FOR ATHENS...

Paul's speech to the Areopagus in Acts 17 is perhaps the finest example of culturally attuned preaching in Scripture.[6] In a basically hostile environment, Paul felt distressed but nevertheless acknowledged the religious orientation of his listeners and then went on to explain the gospel in terms they could understand. A knowledge of Old Testament scriptures could no longer be assumed of his audience, so he quoted from their own Greek poets. He never once compromised the gospel message, but rather made the unpalatable understandable. In effect, he was 'reloading' cultural terminology to draw out Christian truths. A skilled piece of cross-cultural communication if ever there was one.

Acts 17 leaves us with at least four principles for cross-cultural communication today:

● good communication is in the language of the receptor culture (v.28)
● good gospel communication truly engages the audience (v.32)

- true gospel communication will radically challenge any culture (v.24)
- true gospel communication will always carry with it the possibility of rejection (v.32).

In the New Testament epistles, there are examples of how the writers were applying the truth of the Christian gospel to the circumstances and culture of the churches to which they were writing. The rampant immorality of Corinth is the classic example of this. From the wider biblical material, at least two patterns emerge as to how the gospel interacts with culture.

In and out

It does appear that in both the New and Old Testaments God often uses people who are in one culture and yet are not truly part of it – people who are in effect bi-cultural. For example, Moses was Hebrew, yet brought up Egyptian; Daniel and Nehemiah trained in Babylonia, but were Jewish. In the New Testament, Paul and Barnabas were clearly bi-cultural. Barnabas was a Levite, but from Cyprus, and Paul had impeccable credentials, both as a Jew and a Roman citizen (Gal. 1:14; Acts 16:37).

In not of

The gospel touches down in the time and space of the Roman Empire, but it refuses to stay there. The gospel tackles the issues of the day in a way that genuinely engages the real world, but at the same time points beyond it.

So, for example, in the teaching of Ephesians 5 and 6 the gospel engages contemporary issues while at the same time bringing implications that go far beyond the norms of the day. Paul tackles everyday relationships, starting where the culture is: 'Slaves, obey your earthly masters'

(6:5); 'Children, obey your parents' (6:1); 'Wives, submit to your husbands' (5:22). However, at the same time the apostle challenges the accepted customs of the culture: 'And masters, treat your slaves in the same way' (6:9); 'Fathers, do not exasperate your children' (6:4); 'Husbands, love your wives, just as Christ loved the church and gave himself up for her' (5:25).

In short, a gospel that engages culture yet at the same time transcends it. A gospel that is in the world, but not of it.

Balancing act

For Christians to deal biblically with the issue of culture, then, requires an exquisite sense of balance. By being either uncritically affirming or unnecessarily negative to the world, we fail to be fully Christian. The obvious danger lurking at every turn is that Christianity can be undermined by culture. The opportunity that opens up before us, though, is that Christianity can redeem culture.

Let us imagine an American who is sent as a missionary to an African country. He will have to ask himself this question: How can I, who am the product of an Anglo-Saxon culture, take the gospel from the Bible, which was written in the cultures of Judaism and the Greco-Roman world, and communicate it to Africans who belong to a third culture, whether of Islam or of an African traditional religion, without either falsifying the message or rendering it unintelligible? It is this interplay between three cultures – the cultures of the Bible, of the missionary and of the hearers – which constitutes the exciting, yet exacting discipline of cross-cultural communication. (John Stott)[7]

Summary

Biblically speaking, culture must be viewed as carrying within it the same inherent tensions as each one of us does. It bears the undeniable imprint of God ('the echoes of Eden', as Donovan put it) but at the same time it bears the corruption and selfishness of the whole of humanity (Rom. 2:3).

'Because man is God's creature, some of his culture is rich in beauty and goodness. Because he is fallen, all of it is tainted with sin and some of it is demonic.'[8]

Yet God is active in history through his people. By speaking into a culture in its own language as Paul did so brilliantly Christians can be part of God's redemption of cultures. We can celebrate and build upon the God-given parts of a culture and the creativity and diversity each people group brings, whilst challenging the corrupted parts of a culture through radically contrasting lives and God's revealed truths.

Biblically speaking though, there is one more piece to the jigsaw of how the gospel relates to culture, and that has to do with the nature of gospel truth itself.

NOTES

1. John Macquarrie, *Principles of Christian Theology* (SCM, 1966)
2. Bosch, *Transforming Mission* (Orbis Books, 2001) pp.16-20
3. The Hittite Suzerain Treaty, for example.
4. Hesselgrave and Rommen, *Contextualization* (Baker Book House, 1992) pp.4–7
5. Gavin Reid, *The Gagging of God* (IVP, 1969)
6. For a detailed treatment of this important passage see 'Athens revisited' ch.28 in Don Carson's book *Telling the Truth* (Zondervan, 2000)
7. John Stott, *Authentic Christianity* (IVP, 1995) p.332
8. The Lausanne Covenant, para.10, quoted in *The Willowbank Report* (LCWE, 1978), p.5

5

To Humbly Go
(Grasping the truth about culture)

I thirst for truth, but shall not reach it until
I reach the source.[1]

What we are able to learn about our own faith and culture
from other cultures is almost entirely determined by our
attitude to truth.

Truth is desperately important for us as Christians.
We believe God himself is Perfect Truth, that the Bible
is inspired truth and that we are to walk in the truth.
Christianity's claims to truth are also the hottest point
of contention with a society that has largely given up on
truth's existence.

Because truth is so important and contentious, we must
be careful to understand how we come to and hold on to
a knowledge of the truth today.

Our starting point is that we can only know anything
about God if he first chooses to reveal himself to us (Is.
43:12; Rom. 1:19). 'The secret things belong to the Lord
our God, but the things revealed belong to us and to our
children for ever' (Deut. 29:29).

All truth, then, is a gift of grace – we only discovered
it because God first chose to disclose it. True Christian
knowledge should therefore be characterised by humility – not the strutting self-importance of so many in the
academic world. Learning is a miracle of grace.

When that humility is lodged firmly in our minds, it
changes the nature of our proclamation. The gospel itself

LEARNING IS A MIRACLE OF GRACE!

is still clearly not negotiable (Jn. 14:6), but our grasp and
understanding of it is.[2] We are finite minds struggling
with the infinite: 'Now we see but a poor reflection as in
a mirror; then we shall see face to face. Now I know in
part; then I shall know fully, even as I am fully known'
(1 Cor. 13:12).

So we enter into conversations about our faith with confidence in truth revealed, but humble about truth expressed. We long for people to come to a saving knowledge of Christ for themselves, while at the same time we are very mindful that we know only in part. In all likelihood we have got some things wrong, and we have things to learn from those with whom we are talking. Such a view brings us to our knees. We have a gospel to tell and it's a matter of life and death, but our mind cannot do justice to its dimensions. How desperately we need the Holy Spirit to lead us into all truth (Jn. 16:13). Indeed, such is the emphasis in both the Old and New Testaments about humility and truth going together (Ps. 25:9; Prov. 11:2; Phil. 2:3; Tit. 3:2; Jas. 3:13) that it is impossible to have truly Spirit-empowered mission without an attitude of humility towards the people we are wanting to reach.

When we have this more Christian attitude towards truth, we understand that God can work in us as well as through us in these encounters with people of other cultures. We are addressed in the gospel by one who is himself the truth. We do not possess it, he seeks to possess us. 'Christ speaks in this dialogue, revealing himself to those who do not know him and correcting the limited and distorted knowledge of those who do.'[3,4]

So can we remain truly biblical and yet still believe that truth about God can be found in other cultures, and even other religions?

John Stott, in his book *Christian Mission in the Modern World*, sums up the biblical material in the following way: 'We therefore do not deny that there are elements of truth in non-Christian systems and vestiges of general revelation of God in nature. What we do deny is that these are sufficient for salvation.' John Stott goes on by quoting from the World Council of Churches at Uppsala:

> The Christian's dialogue with another implies neither a
> denial of the uniqueness of Christ, nor any loss of his own
> commitment to Christ, but rather a genuinely Christian
> approach to others. He must be human, personal, relevant
> and humble. In dialogue we share our common humanity,
> its dignity and fallenness and express our common concern
> for that humanity.[5]

Here lies a critical point in this book. The church of Jesus
Christ has been given the Great Commission, to take the
good news of Jesus to every people group on the planet
and to make disciples. In doing so, we must confront and
challenge what is wrong in every society and stay faithful
to the message of the cross. But we must also be prepared
to learn and adjust our cultural specs. The sum total of
God's revealed truth does not exclusively reside within the
confines of the church (e.g. Gen. 42) but in the one whom
we worship, and he is not confined to the church.

Summary of Section One

We all tend to underestimate how powerful a hold culture
has over us, and as far as the church is concerned, this
attitude has devastating effects on both our discipleship
and our evangelism.

Things do not need to remain as they are, however. By
understanding the balance that the Bible teaches about
culture, by having a more biblical appreciation of truth
and by trying to reach people of a different culture with
the gospel, our own cultural specs can be exposed, and a
way out of the church's culture trap can be seen.

In Section Two we shall look at whether working with
young people today can really be said to be working with
people of a different culture. If it can, then of course young
people can help lead the church out of its many and various cultural traps.

NOTES

1. Robert Browning
2. A good place to start thinking about the nature of truth in a Christian context is www.faithmaps.org also Don Carson, *Telling the Truth* (Zondervan, 2000)
3. J. Richard Middleton and Brian J. Walsh, *Truth Is Stranger Than It Used to Be* (SPCK), Conclusion
4. For further evidence of the importance of the relationship between mission and dialogue for theology see William D. Taylor, *Global Missiology for the 21st Century* (Baker Books, 2000) p.300 quoting McGrath
5. The World Council of Churches, Uppsala

SECTION TWO

Young People – Are They Really a Different Culture?

Introduction

The world that shapes and influences teenagers of today is so vastly different from the world that shaped and influenced the average church leader of today that communication between the two must bridge a cultural chasm as broad as that tackled by the pioneers of Western mission in the last century.

Over the top? Can we really believe that teenagers today, living in the same town, speaking the same language, even part of the same family, should be understood as a different cultural group?

Well, let's see…

Beware of Monty Python!

One of my favourite comedy sketches is 'We were poor' by Monty Python. In it, each of the characters tries to outdo the other by exaggerating the level of their childhood poverty, with quite hilarious results.

When I read some articles today on contemporary culture, I think the authors would do well to watch Monty Python. They write as if today's young people are the only ones in the whole of history to live under the threat of physical violence, to be left picking up the pieces of their parents' foolishness, and to struggle with confused signals from a society that has lost direction.

We are on shaky ground if each generation of youth workers sees it as their responsibility to show why their generation is worse off than any other. For one thing it is probably not true, and besides, there is a bit of Monty Python in all of us and we don't want our generation to be outdone in its perceived hardships.

My purpose here is not to make value judgements about whether today's teenagers are better or worse off. It is simply to say that they have important differences from other generations, to the extent that it is right and fair to view them as a different cultural group.

Different stages

Not that this is intended, of course, to give the impression that all teenagers can be treated as one group. It is blatantly obvious that a boy in Year Nine struggling with early physical changes is very different from the girl in the sixth form whose independence and identity are much more established. Nor do they all have the same perspectives and worldviews at a particular age. Here lies yet another challenge to those working with teenagers. Not only are they a separate cultural group from adults in society, but at different stages they are distinct from each other.

Nevertheless, there are three ways in which, I believe, teenagers today can be broadly understood to be different:

- in the way they are generally different from adults
- in the way today's experience of adolescence is very different from the experience of previous generations of teenagers
- in the way they are the ones most affected by a changing world.

Over the next three chapters we are going to look at each one of these in a little more detail.

6

Life Spent in Front of the Mirror
(How young people are generally
different from adults)

Peer pressure

I used to drive a Talbot Samba. One day I was giving three
lads a lift home from football when they all dived down
behind the front seat. It had the effect of making it look
as if I was the only one in the car.

Concerned that they might be in some kind of trouble,
I asked the reason for their behaviour, and got a straight
answer: 'Those lads back there go to our school and we
wouldn't be seen dead in a car like this!' That was it.
There was only one thing for it. I reversed down the street,
wound down the window and shouted at the gang on the
corner, 'Have you seen who I've got in my car?'

If I had accepted the frantic promises coming from
the floor of my Talbot Samba over the next few seconds,
I would have inherited the collective wealth of three
families. As I drove off, having spared their blushes
after all, you would have thought that I had just saved
their lives.

Peer pressure is the social and inner pressure to live up to the expectations of others in order to gain their acceptance and approval. It takes up huge amounts of a teenager's time and emotional energy. Sometimes teenagers try so hard to be in with the rest that they end up pretending to be what they are not and enjoying what they obviously don't.

It is not that adults don't suffer from peer pressure (as every parent knows), but it is the sheer brazenness and intensity of the adolescent peer group that sets them apart. Peers should not be confused with friends (at least as adults understand them). Friends, by most definitions, are accepting and tolerant. In a peer group you are only as good as your last performance. It is an uncomfortable place to be. 'Young people try to get by with a little help from their peers. They form their tribal patterns with their own rituals and codes of behaviour. It doesn't really work, but it is better than nothing.'[1]

Young people, collectively at least, tend to value their independence, keep their distance and remain separate from the adult world of their parents. In doing so, they usually end up forming groups. Groups of teenagers operate around a common image and a common stock of information. Conforming to that image and knowledge of that information propels group members up or down the pecking order. The image and information can be anything – a label, a band, a team, a sport, a computer – anything that acts as a social glue to the group involved.

In their own world

Teenage groups often tend to shut out the adult world by keeping their world a very private one. The more it belongs to them, the less it belongs to adults. It is not uncommon for these groups to share values that are frowned upon by the adult world (for example – while parents value hard work, many teenagers value dossing; while adults encourage responsibility, many teenagers try to avoid it). Groups of teenagers often seek to shock the adult world, implicitly communicating through their music, fashion and language that they want their own space.

The point is, even if teenagers eventually grow up to be not too dissimilar from their parents, most adolescents, at one time or another, want to be seen and understood as very different and often distant from their parents' adult world.

Life spent in front of the mirror

According to respected educationalist David Day, teenagers are preoccupied with three basic questions:

LIFE SPENT IN FRONT OF THE MIRROR ...

Do I like myself? Can I manage? Am I an individual? In other words, a preoccupation with themselves and their emerging identity.[2] Puberty only serves to sharpen this focus. Along with developing adult bodies they get the physical and emotional debris of change – greasy hair, spots, a breaking voice, periods. This would be bad enough at the best of times, but when it is experienced against the backdrop of an appearance-obsessed media culture it makes life in front of the mirror uncomfortable and school showers a depraved form of torture.

Of course insecurities carry over into adulthood, but the unique physical and emotional changes of adolescence, the anxiety they create, and the thought, time and energy (not to mention money) they eat up make for major differences between teenagers and adults. This fundamentally affects the way they perceive themselves and the way they are communicated with.

Language

Further raising the cultural barrier between young people and adults is language. Most attempts at cross-cultural communication collide with a language barrier, and working with teenagers is no exception.

Any use of language depends on words having an agreed meaning, and with many of today's teenagers this simply doesn't exist. The meaning of a word changes over time. 'The ideal of timeless English is sheer nonsense. No living language can be timeless. You might as well ask for a motionless river.'[3] English has changed so much that 'in today's world Shakespeare would be a semi-literate.'[4]

This evolving of language is, to a major extent, driven by young people themselves as they use words to establish their distinctive group identity. 'Many youth subcultures identify words which are keys into the culture. These words act as luggage in which young people pack all their subcultural belongings and say this is home.'[5]

Popular slang is often regional of course, but some currently in wider usage include bling-bling, mint, phat, lush, kerching, and respect![6]

This exclusivity of language can cause big problems in the church as our words can unintentionally send the message that young people are not at home with us.

YOUR HEART IS NOT SUFFICIENT
IF YOUR LIPS GET IN THE WAY...

I have listened to you chatting, preacher, chatting from the heart,
But didn't dig your message, 'cos you lost me at the start.
I'm sure you said them from your heart, the things you had to say,
But heart is not sufficient if your lips get in the way.[7]

Understanding language when working with young people is difficult. For one thing, it changes too fast. At least traditional missionaries normally know when they aren't being understood. Sadly, many involved in youth mission today don't realise they are speaking a different language.

Summary of Chapter 6

Looking at the very general, obvious differences between teenagers and adults, their cultural specs are plain to see. But there is much more than this to understanding young people as a new cultural group.

NOTES

1. John Ellis in Michael Eastman (ed.), *Inside Out* (Falcon Press, 1976), p.25
2. David Day, Address to CYFA leaders 1989
3. C. S. Lewis, *Letters to Malcolm* (Collins, 1963). Quoted by John Stott, *Christian Mission in the Modern World* (Kingsway, 1986), p.13
4. Alvin Toffler, *Future Shock* (Bodley Head, 1970), quoting Stuart Berg Flexner, senior editor of the Random House Dictionary of the English Language. Learn about the evolution of the English Language and local dialects www.bbc.co.uk/radio4/routesofenglish/ or for a more lighthearted approach translate your chosen phrase into different British dialects at www.whoohoo.co.uk/
5. Terry Dunnel, 'Spirituality, Culture and Young People' in *Frontier Youth Magazine*
6. news.bbc.co.uk/2/hi/uk_news/education/3135441.stm viewed on 13/8/03
7. Gordon Bailey in Gaukroger and Cohen, *How to Close Your Church in a Decade* (Scripture Union, 1992), p.100

You Were Never Their Age
(How the experience of adolescence is
different today from previous generations)

The trouble is, if we leave it there most adults instinctively
feel that to communicate with this generation is just a question of remembering back to when they were teenagers. We
naively talk about a generation gap as if the only difference
is the year on the calendar. The truth is that even in my
generation (and I am thirty-nine) we were not young like
they are young today. We were never their age.

You never had that body

'Better diet makes bigger people quite quickly. "The few"
would be fewer still today. If the RAF had to put modern
pilots into Spitfires and Hurricanes the majority would not
be able to fit behind the joy stick!'[1]

Teenagers today are maturing earlier physically. There
is evidence to suggest that changes in environment, diet
and medical care have resulted in the onset of puberty
reaching girls as young as nine and ten, and boys at ten
and eleven. Literally, such individuals become children

with adult bodies. This inevitably has significant effects on their behaviour, the way they dress, the way they respond to authority and discipline, the sports they play and not least, of course, their sexual experimentation.

THE GENERATION GAP IS MORE THAN THE YEARS IN BETWEEN ...

You were never that sexy

With adult bodies coming along sooner into a media world that uses sex as its number one attention grabber, into a culture where access to relationships with the opposite sex is more relaxed than at any previous time in recorded history and moral guidance is almost negligible, is it any wonder that sexual activity is more widespread among younger teenagers than perhaps ever before?

The Trust for the Study of Adolescence (TSA) provides statistical evidence that young people are engaging in sexual activity at an earlier age than ever before – 28 per cent of boys and over 19 per cent of girls having had their first experience of intercourse before their sixteenth birthday.[2]

---

39 per cent of men and 27 per cent of women aged 16–19 had two or more sexual partners in 2001/2. 32 per cent of men were virgins at the age of 20.[3]

You were never so old so young

'We are finally learning, though with some regret, that all the problems and issues that filled high school programming a decade ago, must now become the subject of junior high programmes and 10–13-year-olds.'[4]

With physical maturity arriving earlier; with our information society making young people more broadly aware of the world than ever before; with earlier sexual encounters; with our education system giving important decisions to teenagers as young as thirteen; with large amounts of unsupervised free time and many finding part-time work it is little wonder that social commentators refer to the 'erosion of childhood'. The pressure is on to grow up quicker, and though the consequences of this early exposure to the adult world are not yet clear one thing is for sure: people get 'older' younger these days.

You were never so young for so long

Here lies an interesting fault line in our cultural experience. On the one hand, parents encourage the more rapid passing of childhood because, in so many ways, more adult behaviour makes their parental role easier. On the other hand, with a general atmosphere of uncertainty, people fight shy of commitment and the responsibility traditionally associated with adult life. At the same time, governments encourage further education and the marketing world continues to hold out the young, free and single lifestyle as the most fulfilling. The net result? An adolescence which starts earlier and finishes later than it ever did before.

You were never that influential

This in turn gives teenagers influence. A market that grows at both ends means that more resources are spent on gaining its attention, and when the combined forces of the fashion and music industries, the computer and literary worlds, and the leisure conglomerates, to name but a few, bombard the market-place with adolescent-friendly images and products they begin to shape and change the nature of society itself. Respectable adult fashion houses upgrade the chic boutique styles, mainstream musicians add a subtle house beat to make their music more youth friendly and, lo and behold, we all want to be young again.

You never changed so fast

Here lies one of the forces of constant change in the music and fashion industries. Teenagers see themselves as dif-

ferent from adults, and what is more want to be seen as
different. So when adult culture mimics adolescent trends,
it is time for the young to move on. This makes the teenage
market turbulent and fickle. 'If it is in, you can be sure
it is on its way out!' It's a world constantly reinventing
itself – an ever moving target. All in all, it is a gift for the
advertisers as they always have a new product to sell.

ADULT CULTURE MIMICS ADOLESCENT TRENDS...

You never had so many choices

This in turn has led to a fragmenting of adolescent culture. Driven by the ad men's need to sell and the teenage
imperative to make a strong statement, such previously
clear distinctions as either Mod or Rocker have shattered
into a confusing array of choices:

'Choice is a core value for young people now. Young
people are prepared to live with the anxiety of having

choice in order to keep their options open and avoid commitment.'[5]

The irony is that when faced with so many choices today we often fail to make any distinctive choices at all.

You were never that troubled

There can be little doubt that today's teenagers live with the consequences of a society that has lost direction.

- 39 per cent of 15-year-olds reported using illegal drugs in 2001[6]
- 26 per cent of 11–15-year-olds drink at least once a week – the median number of units drunk rose from 5.4 in 1990 to 9.8 units per week in 2001[7]
- Suicide is the third highest killer amongst young people aged 15–35 and the sixth highest cause of death amongst children aged 5–14.[8]

As far as teenage crime is concerned, the picture is far from encouraging. 'Every known factor associated with teenage crime is escalating. Unless we address the issues, our prospects as a peaceful country are terrible beyond measure.'[9]

One cannot help being reminded of Schlossberg's famous quote: 'A society that cannot tolerate a judge beyond history, will find that it can tolerate anything else.'

Summary of Chapter 7

There is much more to the generation gap than the years in between. Today's experience of adolescence is very different from my generation's. I was never fourteen like they are fourteen and it stands to reason that their cultural specs will be different from mine as a result.

NOTES

1. *Daily Telegraph,* October 1996 quoted in *The Week Magazine,* 12 October 1996, p.14
2. John Coleman, *Key Data on Adolescence* (TSA Ltd., 1997), p.50
3. www.doh.gov.uk/HPSSS/TBL_A15.HTM viewed 3/8/03
4. 'Reaching Young People of a Younger Age' – A Youth For Christ Triennial Convocation, 1994
5. Zygmunt Bauman quoted in *Johnny Baker,* 2001 www.cix.co.uk/~pb/natcons2002/baker.pdf. Viewed 3/8/03
6. Department of Health, 2002, www.doh.gov.uk/public/sb0215.htm. Viewed on 03/08/03
7. Department of Health, 2002 www.doh.gov.uk/public/sddsurvey01.htm Viewed on 03/08/03
8. www.about-teen-depression.com/depression-statistics.html Viewed on 03/08/03
9. Masuel M. Haghughi, Honorary Professor of Psychology at Hull University, writing in *The Independent,* April 1993

8

Postmodern Puppets
(How today's teenagers are most influenced
by a changing world)

> Every few hundred years throughout western history, a
> sharp transformation has occurred. In a matter of decades,
> society altogether rearranges itself. ... Fifty years later,
> a new world exists and the people born into that world
> cannot even imagine the world in which their grandparents
> lived. ... Our age is such a period of transformation.[1]

Human nature has not suddenly changed at the beginning of the twenty-first century. The joys and tensions of
adolescence are still basically the same. What has clearly
changed, however, is the environment in which teenage
years are lived out. With a very different kind of culture
surrounding them, there is evidence to suggest that today's
teenagers will grow up with a different set of cultural
specs to our own.

So let us take a brief look at the changing world today's
teenagers live in. First, though, it is important to recognise
that the issues I raise here do not affect teenagers alone.
To some extent they affect every generation in twenty-first
century Britain. My point, though, is that teenagers are

more influenced by them. While the winds of change may buffet older generations, the younger generation can be swept off their feet. To put it another way, when the dust settles after cultural change it is just another layer for adults who have lived through change before. For young people growing up, though, it is the very soil in which they have their roots. It shapes and determines who they are. In short, living in today's climate has more effect on young people's cultural specs than it does on ours. They do not have anything to compare it with.

Cultural Attitudes

Life in the present tense

Take global energy policy as an example. The world needs to reduce carbon dioxide emissions by 60 per cent to reach sustainable levels for the environment, yet the 1998 Kyoto Protocol offers only 5.2 per cent over 20 years because, in the words of US President George W. Bush, 'we will not do anything that harms our economy'.[2]

Take transport in Britain. There is no coherent policy because a government that wanted to be re-elected could never challenge our 'right' to drive our cars 200 metres up the road.

Look at our credit cards. In February 2003, the amount of consumer credit outstanding was £158 billion or about £3,400 for each adult in the UK.[3]

THE FUTURE WHISPERS WHILST THE PRESENT SHOUTS ...

We are ... in the process of endangering the future for our children, yet nobody is doing anything about it. Why not? Because genuine political dialogue has been almost completely replaced by high stakes competition for the ever-shorter attention span of the electorate. The future whispers while the present shouts. Somehow, we have convinced ourselves that we care far less about what happens to our children than about avoiding the inconvenience and discomfort of paying our own bills. So instead of accepting responsibility for our choices, we simply dump huge mountains of both debt and pollution on future generations.[4]

'Capitalism has led to the throwing out
of the principle of housekeeping and fair
distribution. Exponential growth is the
basic law of economics, within no limits.
It is growth for growth's sake. There is no
overarching purpose. A minority is urged to
multiply its wants. The majority lacks basic
needs of existence and the whole economic
system is threatened. If it was in a human
body, they would call it cancer.'[5]

The problems facing our world seem so huge and the
political response so minimal that for today's teenagers the
only solution seems to be not to think beyond the now.

A Life Of Mistrust

"Mistrust, it seems is now directed not just at those
clearly in breach of law and accepted standards, not just
at crooks and wide boys. Mistrust and suspicion have
spread across all areas of life, and supposedly with good
reason. Citizens, it is said, no longer trust governments,
or politicians, or ministers, or the police, or the courts, or
the prison service. Consumers, it is said, no longer trust
business, especially big business, or their products. None
of us, it is said, trusts banks, or insurers, or pension providers. Patients, it is said, no longer trust doctors (think of
Dr Shipman!), and in particular no longer trust hospitals
or hospital consultants. 'Loss of trust' is in short, a cliché
of our times."[6]

Teenagers are particularly vulnerable to our culture of
suspicion. They have never known a time when government ministers were perceived as honest (Clement Atlee in

the 1940s was renowned for his honesty), or public servants were trusted to get on with their jobs without a watchdog looking over their shoulders. Rightly or wrongly we have no faith in public institutions we have to deal with every day, and our teenagers naturally develop critical specs.

Life with disposable choices

Today everybody wants to be free and they measure freedom in choices. What we choose, it seems, is not as important as actually having the freedom to choose.

An increase in choice and change leads to a decrease in commitment and continuity. Choices are seen like a Kleenex tissue, not a silk hankie. Like cups, pens and cameras, they are disposable. Marriages, beliefs and homes – it doesn't matter if something breaks because there is always another one. In such a transient society nothing can be valued.[7]

Freedom is not about having choices, though. Freedom is about making the right choices. Once again, it is young people who pay a heavy price when society gets this wrong.

Zygmunt Bauman describes us as vagabonds. Nomads have purpose, pilgrims have a destination, but disillusionment with the present is all that drives the vagabond on.[8]

Cultural Foundations

Happy families?

Today's teenagers are living through a period of history when society is in danger of losing its family structure. Twenty-three per cent of families with children are lone-parent families today compared with 12 per cent in 1981.[9] Between 1991 and 2001 there were almost 1.2 million divorces in England and Wales.[10]

Disruption to the family (which after all is the anchor of any society) has far-reaching consequences. Many children are left without any model of a lasting committed relationship between adults and their trust in people is damaged by parents who are perceived to have walked out on them.

> Divorce is associated with more adverse outcomes for children than the death of a parent, and the remarriage of a parent appears in some circumstances to add to the children's difficulties. Our findings are supported by a very large body of research of many different kinds.[11]

For families still together, things have also changed. It is also hard for the latchkey generation, children who let themselves in after school and heat up their tea while their parents work shifts. And for the 'absence makes the heart go purchasing' crowd, whose earning parents make up for a lack of time with an abundance of presents. A November 2000 poll reveals that 'a large majority of the children (70 per cent) say it's important for parents to get on well together if they are to raise happy children. However, just a third of parents share that view.'[12]

The School Years

Few experiences have more impact on the colour of our cultural specs than our formal education – not simply what we learn, but also how we learn it.

Facts are no longer given to be recorded and then at a later date regurgitated. Today the world of indisputable facts has become decidedly smaller. The emphasis is on discovering, evaluating and questioning a wealth of sources and perspectives, but only ever reaching tentative conclusions. Teenagers become accustomed to testing and checking everything and everyone.

Managed Schools – Manufactured Specs

Management of education in this country is experiencing huge changes with far reaching consequences for all pupils within the education system.

The introduction of SATs and Ofsted inspections means children and teachers are more target orientated. From the age of seven, pupils now have to sit exams. One survey shows that 80 per cent of Year 2 and 3 pupils feel stress due to schoolwork.[13] With so much resting on SAT results there is a growing concern that the broader elements of the curriculum are being neglected by teachers to improve the measurements that matter to Ofsted inspectors.

When I was in the 6th form I felt part of a tangible community. I had a tutor group I met with each day, and there were lunchtime and after-class activities as well as a great common room. Some years later I worked with sixth form students at Luton. They had to wear swipe ID cards to convince uniformed security men of their right to be there. Staggered lunch breaks meant virtually all lunchtime clubs had closed and there weren't enough desks for all the students.

Far from encouraging community responsibility and citizenship, current management practice in education is shaping an individualistic generation of adults who see themselves as clients and the state as provider.

Cultural Experience

Total media exposure

Today's media world is intrusive. Every waking moment it competes for our attention through one form or another. Teenagers are especially vulnerable to such bombardment.

THE HEAVY BIT

'The various forms of media are the icons of our society. Through them we see what we want to value and esteem, by them we make choices. In the matrix of our experience and what we watch or listen to, our views and values are shaped. Then in turn it is with those opinions and values that we perceive, interpret and discern our world, our context.'[14]

Advertising

Advertising might not be new, but its intrusion into our daily lives is immeasurable – product placement, television, radio, magazines, newspapers, billboards, flyers,

HAPPINESS = CONSUMPTION

spam, banners, pop-ups. It is such a part of everyday life we don't notice it, or at least we don't think we do.

Teenagers are to be forgiven for assuming they were born to shop or that happiness equals consumption. Advertisers no longer sell products, but a whole set of values that create a community through consumerism.

Renzo Rosso, the owner of Diesel Jeans, explains: 'We don't sell a product, we sell a way of life. I think we have created a movement. ... The Diesel concept is everything. It's the way to live, it's the way to wear, it's the way to do something.'[15]

It is working. In 2002 alone, tweens (8–14-year-olds) spent or influenced the spending of an estimated $1.18 trillion worldwide on everything from shoes to their parents' car.[16]

The tactics of brand managers become ever more sophisticated. Take the Matrix films. In the months surrounding each release it permeated every area of a teenager's life – fast food, the computer game, cars, internet sites, chat rooms, blogs, shades, philosophical discussion, mobile phones and clothing, not to mention the steady stream of carefully placed media adverts, reviews and discussions. A plethora of seemingly unrelated products were 'situated' within the Matrix brand in order to cash in on this huge event. Paradoxically, although older teenagers are very brand savvy, even if they are aware of marketing strategies the sheer force of cultural reshaping engulfs them.[17]

Huge budgets are devoted to an unscrupulous play upon human emotions and frailties. As marketing departments become increasingly sophisticated at targeting specific groups and individuals, they become more adept at exploiting our desires, weaknesses, guilt feelings and fallibilities.

'Malls are the cathedrals of late modernity, where people come to gaze and wonder in the sacred space, to offer homage and pay their dues to the gods of mammon.'[18]

Magazines

Big business is competing ferociously for advantage in the huge and lucrative market for teenage magazines. All that matters is what sells, so teenage magazines tend to slump to the lowest common denominator. Outside of the special interest titles, the important things tend to be the overall image and impression of the magazine's design, the fashion pages, the media star gossip and lots and lots of sex. They are, in other words, designed to please at the shallowest levels. 'Watch a teenage girl going through her favourite magazine. She is comparing herself to images, imagining herself with certain products displayed, comparing male portraits to her own fantasies, and in general being instructed as to how she can better live her life socially. In effect, she is having her cultural quiet time.'[19]

Television

'The average teenager watches 28 hours of TV a week and the average working person 18 hours a week. By the time you are 60 you have spent nine years in front of the television. That changes the way we see the world.'[20]

Part of the problem is that younger people are not critical media consumers. They struggle to distinguish between the projected image and its underlying message.

When the head of MTV, Ben Johnson, was interviewed

by Tony Campolo, he was asked, 'How do you seek to
influence teenagers?' His reply was stark: 'We don't seek
to influence them, we own them.' He went on to say that
what appeals to kids is a diet of anger and intimacy.[21]

Several commentators make the point that the nature of
story has been changed by our TV culture. Parents used
to tell stories to children, and those stories were imbibed
with their own values and worldviews. Today's parents,
though, often take the easy option and delegate storytelling to the television, without ever really thinking through
the values and motives of the programme makers.[22]

With increasing evidence that the nine o'clock watershed means nothing for children with televisions in their
bedrooms, the debate staggers on about how TV viewing
shapes the way we behave. Surely even in these confused
times we are able to see this one clearly. If what we watch
does not influence, at least in part, the way we behave then
why do corporations spend billions of pounds every year
on television advertising?

It is not only the content of programmes, though, that
is of concern. It is also the nature of the communication
itself. Some argue that what teenagers gain in visual
sophistication, they lose in their ability to communicate.
Others see exposure to television as undermining the
nature of reality itself.

To go straight from Iraq to Big Brother, to be treated as
having a two-minute attention span, to be assumed to
need more and more stimulation by increasingly startling
presentations, to be bombarded by a succession of
instantaneous experiences, to be endlessly diverted, to have
no time to pause and reflect, is to have everything reduced
to the same level of significance – or insignificance.[23]

The task of all parents in the media age must be to teach their children that watching television is a cultural exercise and must be done selectively, for every day it shapes the way we perceive reality.

Personal Communications

The internet and mobile phones have added to the 'now' culture of teenagers. Technology enables people to be more spontaneous and instant than ever before. Why plan ahead or take a map if you can ring when you get there? Waiting and patience are disciplines that no longer have to be practised. Nor does storytelling; texting either in words or pictures sees to that. We don't need to hear the story – we can experience it with them. It's life at breakneck speed.

> Over the last two decades there has been a million-fold improvement in computing power. A task that took one year to complete twenty years ago now takes thirty seconds. By 2020 it is estimated that there will be another 4000-fold increase in power.[24]

The last word in this chapter goes to respected theologian David Bosch: 'The point is simply that the Christian church in general and Christian mission in particular are today confronted with issues they had never even dreamt of and which are crying out for responses that are both relevant to the times and in harmony with the essence of the Christian faith.'[25]

Summary of Section Two

Given all that we have read over the last three chapters, it is little wonder that the Anglican Church report 'Youth Apart' drew the following conclusion: 'The primary frontier which needs to be crossed in mission to young people is not so much a generation gap, as a profound change in the overall culture.'

Here lies the heart of this book. This is what motivates me to write.

It is legitimate to say that young people today are a different cultural group. That means the church of Jesus Christ has things to challenge in youth culture if it is to be faithful to the gospel. Critically, though, it also has things to learn from young people. At the moment, this rarely, if ever, happens, and both the church and young people are more impoverished as a result.

The rest of this book goes on to outline some of the lessons the church can learn by taking young people seriously, and to explore how the church can be led out of its culture trap by working with and listening to teenagers.

I am reminded of David Pawson speaking on the story of Samson. The once mighty judge of Israel was now an impotent, stumbling shadow of his former self. At last trusting in God alone, he asked a young boy to guide him to the centre of the Philistine temple, and in one final incredible display of strength, God's enemies were defeated. Possibly God will do it again, Pawson ventured. This time the slumbering giant of the church, stripped of every security save its faith in God, will be brought to the centre of our nation's life to display his power, and perhaps again he will use young people to do it.

Notes

1. Peter Drucker, *Post Capitalist Society* (Butterworth/ Heinemann), p.16
2. Intergovernmental Panel on Climate Change in Christian Aid's *'The Kyoto Climate Fraud – What's wrong with the Kyoto Protocol?, a developing country perspective'* section 2.2, 2000. Viewed at www.christian-aid.org.uk/indepth/0010hagu/hague2.htm#2 on 25/08/03; George W Bush in *'ENVIRONMENT: US Economy Comes First, Says Bush'*, Interpress Service, at www.oneworld.org/ips2/mar01/22_46_082.html 29 March 2001. Viewed on 25/08/03
3. Office of National Statistics Dataset – Consumer Credit Business in *'In too deep'* CAB p.8 May 2003
4. Vice President Al Gore, *Earth in the Balance* (Plume Books), p.170
5. Lesslie Newbigin, *Foolishness to the Greeks* (SPCK, 1985), ch.5
6. Onora O'Neill, *A Question of Trust*, Reith Lectures 2002, Lecture no 1 www.bbc.co.uk/radio4/reith2002/3a
7. This is the argument of Os Guinness, *The Gravedigger File* (Hodder & Stoughton, 1983), p.101
8. Zygmunt Bauman quoted by Roy McLoughry, *Tomorrow's People* (Christian Institute Lectures , 1996)
9. Average (mean) number of dependent children by family type: 1971 to 2001: Living in Britain www.nationalstatistics.gov.uk viewed 15/8/03
10. www.nationalstatistics.gov.uk Divorces: age and sex (England and Wales): Population Trends 112
11. M. P. M. Richards, *Parental Divorce and Children*, LJRC data, Archive Bulletin no. 51, September 1992
12. Mori Poll, November 2000 www.mori.com/polls/2000/nfpi.shtml, viewed 03/08/03
13. *'Stressed at seven? A survey into the scandal of SATs for 7 year olds'* Liberal Democrats, May 2003
14. Gavin McGrath, NB Magazine (UCCF), issue 4
15. Naomi Kline, *No Logo* (Flamingo 2000), p.23
16. Martin Lindstrom, www.dualbook.com/aboutbc.php, viewed 15/08/03

17. Branding guru Martin Lindstrom notes: "53% of all kids worldwide are stressed and are looking towards brands, which can help them enjoy their lives better and that 56% of kids worldwide are looking for a religion, which can make them happy. [My book] BRANDchild explores how religious issues are going to become part of future brand building techniques." (www.dualbook.com/aboutbc.php) Finally he adds: "Due to September 11th, safe values are more hip than ever." It is highly irrational, while paradoxically being highly effective.

18. Andrew Walker, *Telling the Story: Gospel Mission and Culture* (SPCK), quoted in Leading Light Magazine, vol. 3/1, Summer 1996

19. Dean Borgman, *Youth Culture and the Media*, Perspectives (Baptist Youth Ministry Magazine), issue 13, Spring 1995

20. S. Gaukroger and Cohen, *How to Close Your Church in a Decade* (Scripture Union, 1992), p.80

21. Phil Wall, *The Exodus of the Young*, Salvationist Magazine

22. Researching TV habits amongst children from 1996–2001, Kam Atwal found: "The children in our study couldn't imagine life without it. Some were amazed that turning off the television might be a consideration." www.literacytrust.org.uk/database/media.html#constant, published 2003, viewed 03/08/03

23. Adapted from Dr John Habgood, *Culture of Contempt*, in Leading Light Magazine, Vol. 3/1, Summer 1996, p.7.

24. Bill Gates, *Creating the Global Information Society*, a Microsoft White Paper, 1995, p.7. And David Triesman, *Britain in 2020*, (Forethought, July 2003). Introduction viewed at www.labour.org.uk/britainin2020/ on 25/8/03

25. David Bosch, *Transforming Mission* (Orbis, 2001) p.188

SECTION THREE

Essential Youth

Introduction

During my ten years in youth ministry, I never faced a problem in the youth programme that did not have a parallel in the history of the wider church. For a variety of reasons (to do with size, lack of tradition and the flexibility of the people involved), these problems are easier to address in the youth ministry context.

Here lies the heart of this final section. Leadership strategies that are pioneered in the youth group have something to teach the wider church. If it is good practice with young people, it is good practice with the adult congregation too.

So what can we learn?

9

Evangelistic Essentials

'The church that turns in on itself is no longer a church.'[1]

We saw in Chapter 2 that the basic problem with evangelism today is twofold:

1. We are failing to take seriously the cultural setting of the·people we are trying to reach.
2. In trying to reach them, we are encumbered by a church culture which is out of tune with the rest of society.

Let us see how working with young people helps the church in its evangelistic task.

'To evangelise is to proclaim God's good news about Jesus Christ, to the end that people will believe in him, find life in him and ultimately be conformed to his image, not ours.'[2]

The story behind the headlines

A church once asked me to act as a youth consultant. From the outside, everything looked fine. It was larger than average, it had a good number of young families, and it had an effective and efficient leadership team. The problem was the young people – at least that's what they said. There just weren't any. They attended the mid-week clubs, but despite several attempts to encourage them they would not come to the services.

I met with the minister and then separately with all the other leaders involved so that they could tell me what they really felt the problems were. Needless to say, all of them had their own theories and their own angle on things. The youth leaders were clear that the services were too long and boring, and that the teaching and music style failed to engage with adolescents, while one of the elders confided in me that if only there was better Bible teaching and less entertainment in the youth programme, the problems with young people would not exist in the first place.

Finally, the night arrived to meet with them all together. Everybody in the room was focussed on the problem of the young people. I was about to disappoint them.

I began with a question: 'When was the last time you saw an adult converted from a non-Christian background?' Everybody looked a bit puzzled – after all, we were here to talk about teenagers. Following some discussion, it was agreed that they could only remember one man and he had come to faith a few years previously. An embarrassed silence fell upon the room as the truth began to sink in. I put up an OHP slide: 'This church does not have a problem with young people. Fundamentally, this church has a problem with the gospel!'

As any counsellor will tell you, the first problem that people start talking about is rarely the real issue. The presenting problem is often little more than a doorway to the root issue itself. So it is with young people in the church. They are often presented as the problem, but rarely the root of the problem. Young people are a sensitive thermometer to an ice-age church, however much youth leaders might try to warm things up. They are often the first to feel the chill of cultural irrelevance; the first to feel left out in the cold by a church obsessed with looking inwards. So they leave – on a national scale and in their droves. But when they do, it is a symptom of the cancer in church life – not the tumour itself. Basically, the church does not have a problem with young people. It has a problem with the gospel.

Think about it logically. Teenagers are in all likelihood the single largest group of non-Christians who regularly attend your church activities. For a church whose faithfulness to God is at least in part measured by its attempts to reach the lost, doesn't that make what they think and like important?

If we approach youth work from this perspective, what else is there to learn about the church's evangelistic task?

Cultural captives

Working with young people quickly exposes the church's cultural blind spots.

Every Sunday it happens up and down the country: teenagers behaving inappropriately in church. It becomes almost a ritual as both sides take it as far as they can without actually disrupting the service. On the one hand, teenagers might talk, fidget, pass round sweets, go to the toilet, giggle, even fight, but normally to a level that lets everyone know they are there, rather than cause an outright interruption to proceedings. On the other side, the valiant youth leaders glare, have quiet words during hymns, bribe, prod, and move next to the young people concerned, again while not actually halting proceedings with an outright confrontation. In its simplest terms, it is a game of dare and brinkmanship

I have played for both sides more times than I care to remember, and I've found that when teenage attitudes and behaviour are seen as inappropriate for church life it is often more because the way we do church is inappropriate

IN SIMPLEST TERMS IT'S A GAME
OF DARE AND BRINKMANSHIP...

for today's world. Of course, I am not about to condone bad behaviour, but unless we are able to see what it highlights in church practice we are missing what I believe is a God-given opportunity. Much of what we do is boring, many of our practices are outdated and many of our methods don't work, so why do we strenuously resist change? If the only reason is that we are comfortable this way, then the sacrifices demanded by the cross of Christ have been bypassed somewhere along the line.

Here is one of the reasons young people are essential to the church in its evangelistic task. They are a constant reminder that we must be relevant to contemporary society. They are sometimes a God-given thorn in our flesh to teach us that personal preference is not the issue. It is what communicates with the lost that counts.

To dismiss teenagers as loud and abrasive is to miss the fact that the whole of our culture is more and more youth oriented, and it wrongly assumes that because visiting adults don't complain they find our patterns of church appealing and engaging. If that is so, why are they such infrequent attenders?

The uncomfortable truth that the church has to face up to is that however unfair, selfish and mistaken some teenagers' comments about church life are, they nevertheless hit a raw nerve. At the beginning of the twenty-first century, God's people are missing engagement with the world by a very big margin indeed.

Every church struggles to find a service appropriate for everyone. I do not for a moment want to suggest that all services should be youth oriented, and in any case there is no single 'youth culture' to which all teenagers subscribe. Such a service would not only unnecessarily alienate many others in society, but it would sell teenagers themselves short as they too must learn of the personal sacrifices we must all make for the sake of the gospel. If older Christians in church do not model it to them, how will they learn?

'In marketing terms at least "youth" is now a mind-set instead of an age range.'[3]

When we get to know them and spend time with them, teenagers will give us an insight into their immediate and emotional world. It is throbbing with energy and life.

Many a time I have sat in church with them and thought, 'If I am honest, I am bored. No wonder they are struggling.' Yet in other contexts I have been privileged to hear them pray and ask penetrating questions about what the gospel means today, and demonstrate great courage in their faith, all of which reveals a genuine relationship with God. It is at these moments that the cultural captivity of the church becomes clear. There must be more attractive and engaging ways of doing church for people today.

'92 per cent of young people don't come to church because they don't want to. Church is so alien in its dress, language, layout, music, rituals, structure of authority, sexism.'[4]

The real enemy

It was going really well. I had been invited into a local school to answer questions about my faith. The Year 11 class had prepared some good questions and we'd had some fun as we negotiated the usual apologetics issues. As the end of the lesson approached, though, the questions became more personal and honest. It was obvious that a number in the class were genuinely searching. It was a marvellous opportunity as people were prepared to be vulnerable about what was missing in their life.

All too soon the bell went, but as the kids started to pack away their books I still felt excited about the potential of our time together. I was quickly brought back to reality when the teacher closed the lesson. 'Our thanks to Mr. Hickford this morning. As you know, this is the start of our series "What my faith means to me". Next week we have the imam from Bury Park Mosque visiting and the following week we have the rabbi from the synagogue. Your homework for this week is to prepare another set of good questions for the imam. You may go.'

As the class trooped out, now thinking about what they were going to have for lunch, the words of Steve Turner came to mind:

Today we don't stone prophets,
we don't even censor them,
we don't put them in prison,
we just put them in perspective.[5]

When I was at school, there was only one faith I knew anything about. We sang Christian hymns in assembly and despite it being a large, modern comprehensive, we studied Christianity in RE. Awareness and appreciation of people of other beliefs came in social studies, but the thought that what they believed might be of some help to me was never even hinted at. It never entered into my thinking that their faith could be an option for me, or even that it could possibly be true.

Today's multiple choice world is very different. A multi-cultural society demands a multi-faith education. The fascination of our age for the weird and the wonderful helps ensure that we are exposed to an increasing and confusing array of gurus, sects, cults and a whole variety of religious teaching.

'I have travelled the world, searching for something in which to believe. My spiritual journey has involved working with Californian New Age teachers, studying with the Indian and Tibetan holy women and men, being healed by native American shamans, trance dancing to African drums, visiting

> sacred Celtic sites, delving into my Jewish
> roots, studying the power of Kundalini
> energy and sacred Tantric lovemaking,
> learning the power of silence, and going
> inward and celebrating the return of the
> goddess through connection with Mother
> Earth... I am currently practising Raj yoga
> meditation, with the Brahma Kumaris, an
> international spiritual organisation founded
> in India ... I have come a long way from the
> ad fab days, but I'm just a woman on her
> own journey to her truth.'[6]

This class had genuine and searching questions, but over
three weeks they were about to hear three completely
different sets of answers. How could they possibly be
expected to weigh them up and decide what was true?
I thought about it more as I drove home in the car. They
had heard me talk about my personal faith, but that is all
it was to them – my personal faith. The thought that it
might ultimately be true and have huge implications for
them was not likely even to enter their minds.

I believe that there are several things to be learned here
by the wider church.

First, evangelism today has to recognise the competition. In the marketplace of belief, people shop around for
the best bargains on offer and teenagers are growing up
in a DIY society. It is a pick-and-mix arrangement where
nuggets of, say, popular psychology are blended with
traditional Christianity, layered on a base of secularism
and sprinkled with Eastern mysticism.

Christianity is but one of a number of options on offer
from which people can choose what to believe, so the
gospel needs to be compared and contrasted to some of
the other faiths available.

This is not all bad news. While there is little doubt that our postmodern Western society is heading in the opposite direction to the world the Bible writers envisaged, it could be said that it is at the same time becoming more like the world in which the New Testament was originally written. Then as now, Christianity had to compete in the marketplace of belief. Perhaps more so now than for many years there is a direct application of the methods of the early church to our situation today.

In our evangelism, we must recognise the atmosphere created by the sheer number of choices. That these young people had choices about faith was not the problem. After all, if Christianity is true then it can stand up to the toughest competition. The truly awful thing about our society right now is the way that the quantity of choices erodes our confidence in their quality – people can't imagine that any of the choices on offer might actually be true.

Our real enemy is not pluralism. The real enemy is relativism. There is no longer confidence in a public truth that is universal and demonstrable, and so applies to everyone. Truth today is what is true for you – an issue of sincerity, not of clarity. The award winning 1999 Manic Street Preachers album *'This is my truth, now tell me yours'* says it all.

As Clive Calver has written: 'Truth has been lowered to the level of what can be attained, rather than raised to the height of what we must aspire to. Contemporary society has moved one step away from the Garden of Eden. No longer do we reject God's truth, we now deny that it even existed.'[7]

This pragmatic approach is a bit like a Little Chef restaurant. It's an OK place to rest on the journey, but not somewhere you would choose to live. A pragmatic lifestyle might be valid for a time, while trying to find truth, but to stay there for ever, resigned to never finding the meaning to life, is a despairing and empty place to be.

'Pragmatism is the last stand of a culture which has lost its true centre.'[8]

Such a dominant atmosphere requires the church to hold a very delicate balance in its proclamation of the gospel if it is to engage genuinely yet faithfully with our world. On the one hand we worship a God who, the Bible tells us, delights in the truth and personifies and epitomises truth itself.

There can be no compromise here. If the church gives up on Jesus' claim to be the exclusive truth, then we have nothing left to offer. Instead we must be robust in showing the damage that the loss of truth brings to society and

THE NUMBER OF OPTIONS FOR TRUTH HAS ERODED OUR CONFIDENCE IN ANY REAL TRUTH BEING LEFT...

forever refuse to be packaged into the world of private truths only. We must speak out boldly and wisely – in the political arena, in ethical debates and in shaping the future direction of society.

'The loss of truth is absolutely fundamental. Everything flows from that. You reach the point where we are today as Nietzsche predicted, denying that anything can be affirmed as absolutely true. The only way to tackle a society that has jettisoned absolute truth is to tell the whole story and to tell it with confidence ... for if there is no truth we are just adrift in a shoreless ocean.'[9]

On the other hand, we must remember that every culture has something of God's thumbprint inherent in it and Western cultures are no exception. While we must stand against the loss of truth in society, we must also allow something of the evasiveness of truth, of which today's world is so aware, to bring fresh insight into biblical teaching. Evangelicals, for example, are beginning to realise that claims to know absolute truths do not hold water in today's world. Postmodernism has helped to remind us that knowing absolute truth is not a biblical doctrine. Truth is transcendent as he lies beyond us. Truth resides in God, and his ways are greater than ours.

So the great challenge facing the church is to proclaim boldly in the public arena the truth of the gospel with its many implications for society, but with a humility and honest vulnerability which engages a searching world in genuine dialogue.

Truth is stranger than it used to be. Postmodern understanding points us to exciting dimensions of the biblical text of which we were previously unaware.[10]

People, not propositions

Martin appeared to have it all. At sixteen he was head boy, first team football captain, solid academically and with the kind of looks that ensure almost constant female attention.

He was part of a crowd that began to attend a bar we ran, and his natural confidence and social skills meant that we got to know each other quite quickly. It soon became apparent that Martin was a pretty shrewd character. He somehow managed to make everyone feel a valued friend without letting them get close.

As the months passed and we prayed about this group of young people, the issue seemed to be how to move beyond the happy but superficial relationships. The key to that was Martin. Gradually, over a two-year period, trust deepened, conversations about faith took place naturally and we made a point of being as open and honest about our relationships with Christ as we could be.

Eventually, after one meeting, Martin cornered me in a manner much more blunt and direct than usual.

'What would you do if I could disprove Christianity to you?' he asked.

'I would resign,' I said, without really thinking.

'In that case, pray with me. I want to become a Christian,' he replied.

Working with young people like Martin gives the church another insight about how to reach the modern world – it shows the way that truth is arrived at today. Nothing distinguishes better the difference between the modern and postmodern world than their approaches to what is called epistemology, or theories of how truth is established. 'It is not about differences of opinion, but a fundamental difference in the way that opinion is reached.'[11] Understanding that is fundamental to understanding evangelism in today's world.

The church is basically modernist in its understanding. We proclaim the truth of God's word and expect people to respond. But non-Christians think differently. Martin was typically postmodern in his conversion experience. Truth for him was relational and experiential before it was propositional. In other words, he arrived at his decision over a long period of time, and it was through the dynamic of interacting with a group of Christians and trying Christianity out on the quiet rather than being preached a message to which he responded. Objective truth was the last piece of the jigsaw for Martin, not the first.

Here is another doorway to the non-Christian world at large that working with young people provides. People are looking around for what works and crucially they are looking for it in the people around them.

Once again, this postmodern view brings to light elements of biblical teaching that have sometimes been overlooked. It reminds us that our first calling is to follow Christ – to live out something radically different. Rather than simply preach the message, we must first live it.

The world judges Christianity not on apologetics, but on the church.

If this is correct it has huge implications for the way individual Christians live their lives. It is simply not good enough for us to give priority to church activities and pray for people to become Christians. God wants to use us to answer our own prayers. Unless we are giving priority to quality time with non-Christians, how will they ever hear and see the gospel? To pray for revival without making every effort to form genuine friendships with non-Christians is pure escapism.

Sadly, we are very slow to learn. In 1969, Gavin Reid wrote: 'As fishers of men we can no longer wait for the arrival of shoals in carefully built reservoirs and yet we still tie up our people in activities.'[12]

From sex to salvation

Talking to fifteen-year-olds about a Christian view of sex is always a challenging prospect. These days one can't help feeling that it is trying to shut the stable door after the horse has bolted. After all, some of them at fifteen have had more sexual partners than I have.

The one good thing about taking a sex lesson, though, is that most people (particularly at fifteen) are interested in the subject. Imagine my surprise, then, when I was introduced to one class at a local school and a girl in the front row immediately said in a loud voice, 'This is going to be boring. We all know what you are going to say anyway!'

A little taken aback, I said, 'Oh really? Please tell me.'

'You are going to say that it is wrong to have sex and we should wait until we are married,' she said. There were murmurs of support from other members of the class. It was obvious that she was not alone in thinking this way.

'If I promise not to say those things,' I said, 'and I am as honest as I can be about what I think, will you listen to me?'

She gave a cautious OK (which basically meant that I had five minutes to prove myself, otherwise they would all switch off) and the lesson got going.

The first ten minutes looked at our sex-mad society. I had video and music clips, adverts, magazines, etc. We had a laugh at some of the absurd bits and debunked a few of Hollywood's sex myths (which the more sexually experienced in the class were quite open in affirming!). I even managed to demonstrate perfectly why advertisers use sexual imagery when I held up a particular poster and two boys at the back stood up to get a better look. After ten minutes we were at saturation point and some of them were beginning to realise, perhaps for the first time, just how sex mad our contemporary world really is.

Then we moved on to the downside: Society fans the flames without thinking of the consequences. We looked at how many videos have rape scenes to boost their sales, and we read in worksheets of paedophile and abuse rings and the realities of the pornography industry, as well as an article of a girl who fulfilled her dreams and slept with her pop idol with crushing results. We looked at the terrifying reality of sexually transmitted diseases and the nightmare of 4.5 million abortions in the last thirty years. Then to a now hushed class I said: 'And some of us here know from bitter experience how sex is not all it's cracked up to be.'

I talked about some of the fears and motives that drive us into sexual relationships and summed up at the halfway point by saying, 'You can see why I am not satisfied that what we all think about sex actually works.' The class were with me now.

The next part of the lesson looked at some alternative views, contrasting what we labelled the Victorian and the hippie views and trying to see what was good, but also what was weak, about each.

Only after all this did I sense the class were ready to hear what I really thought. I told them that sex was fantastic and that far from being dirty and wrong, when they felt that indescribable excitement of sexual attraction, it was actually a gift from God. I talked about how I believe that we are made in God's image, which means we long to be loved and to be intimate with someone special. I talked about how we have ignored the maker's instructions, and are now reaping the consequences of that; how in today's world we look to sexual partners for what only God can provide. Then with five minutes left I talked honestly about my own struggles with sexuality before giving some practical pointers to people who chose not to sleep around.

'Sex is, I believe, the contemporary religion substitute par excellence. Sex has supplanted religion in the imagination as a favourite way to the beyond. Sex is so often associated with pleasure in the popular press that its links with reproduction are almost forgotten.'[13]

The next day I had a phone call from the teacher. The class had asked her to invite me back the following week. That next lesson, they had an hour's worth of questions ready for me and I tried to answer them as best I could. As a result of that, three of the class asked to see me privately and ended up attending the local church. As for me, the whole episode began to clarify some of what I had been thinking. There are a number of things we can learn from this.

1. People think they know what we want to say, when they don't

Like the girl in the front row, many adults today have a 'been there, got the T-shirt' attitude about Christianity. They remember, perhaps, assemblies at school, scout and guide parades or singing in the choir, supplemented with the odd church christening, wedding and funeral, and they think they have 'done' Christianity. It is all part of being a once-Christian country. People might be more open to spiritual things now, but there is a feeling of having moved on from established Christian religion.

The trouble with that attitude is that the public face of Christian religion so often copies the effect but loses the heart of the gospel. Now we face an uphill task. We have a vital message to tell, but people think they have heard it already, when they have not.

Søren Kierkegaard told the famous story of a clown. Each day he would go to the village and entertain the crowd with his antics. On one occasion, though, he could see that a fire had started behind the crowd. He frantically tried to warn his audience, but they thought it was just part of his show and roared with laughter. As a result, the village burned down. They too thought they knew what the clown was trying to say.

Among young people there is an important difference. The vast majority of teens have not rejected Jesus – they do not know enough about him to have done that. Peter Brierley, in his book *Reaching and Keeping Teenagers*, has shown, however, that they do see going to church as a children's activity enforced by parents, which any self-respecting teenager should have grown out of by now. In this sense, they share with adults a 'we have moved on from there' attitude towards Christianity.

2. *Evangelism has to start further back*

The problem is that we face a generation who are in effect self-destructing while at the same time feeling perversely self-sufficient. To communicate the gospel effectively in this kind of world, we have to take evangelism one step further back. We must recognise that people won't consider Jesus until they discover that what they believe is neither true, nor does it work.

Today's evangelistic process has to begin with exposing the lies of the world in which we live; unmasking the gods of this age, with all their pretence, so that this generation will sense their need to ask the questions that Jesus answers.[14]

3. Evangelism today often begins with issues

Society is interested in movements, not institutions. For example, we have seen the development of single-issue politics in recent years. People don't believe in big, over-arching truths any more, but they will back a cause they believe in. The church needs to be sensitive to this agenda and have a much more flexible view of evangelism. In today's world some of the best opportunities arise out of first proving that Christianity has something helpful and credible to say into the issues of the day. Brian McLaren, author of *A New Kind of Christian*, has spoken of his sadness following the awful events of 11 September when, for many Americans, evangelical leaders interviewed in the national media were worse than the politicians at answering the searching questions of the nation. They preferred instead to take the opportunity to get the message out that everyone needs Jesus as their personal saviour.[15]

Whilst they were faithfully motivated, the tragedy was that once again Christians were retreating to their private world of faith and effectively conceding that in the public realms of foreign and defence policy they had little or nothing to contribute. It was a classic example of what we looked at in Chapter 2. The greatest irony was that in emphasizing Jesus as personal saviour, Jesus as lord was largely ignored.

On the personal level, we need to address what Willow Creek calls the 'felt needs of people' – i.e. handling stress, bringing up our children, balancing the budget, maximising our marriage. If we prove that Christianity has something to say to these contemporary issues, the doorway is open to people's attention. One thing is for sure: if the church is going to respond to young people in today's world, it has to be seen to be responding to sexuality in our culture.

Thom Hopler suggests that history goes in waves and these waves are realities, though they are difficult to pin down in actual years. In the early years of each new wave the missionaries have to be different, e.g. Christian women taken captive by Vikings, William Carey going it alone to India, etc. The early part of any of these waves sees new creative ways of getting the gospel out. We can be paralysed by fear, or we can seek out creative new means of dealing with these movements.

> I don't know what they will look like, but I believe new methods are there to be found by courageous Christians willing to try. We can and must take advantage of the forces that threaten to destroy us and use them to expand and strengthen God's church.[16]

Summary of Chapter 9

The church does not have a problem with young people. The church has a problem with the gospel.

If the church takes the gospel seriously, it will inevitably take young people seriously as they are the single largest group of non-Christians regularly attending church.

When we do take young people seriously the church is helped in overcoming a number of barriers to evangelism in our world today.

- We are forced to recognise our own cultural blindness.
- We learn to preach a gospel more relevant to an issue-dominated society that has lost its grip on truth.

● Most of all we are reminded of the need to live that truth as well as preach it. Like it or not, in the postmodern world the church is the Christian apologetic.

Notes

1. Vincent Donovan, *Christianity Rediscovered* (SCM Press, 1978) p.120
2. John Stott, *Authentic Christianity* (IVP, 1997)
3. *The Face* (March 2000 in Johnny Baker Essay, 2001)
4. Johnny Baker, 'Enculturalising the Gospel' (BYFC Position Paper, 1995)
5. Steve Turner quoted in David Lyon, *The Steeple's Shadow* (SPCK)
6. Lynn Franks in *The Times*, 24 June 1996.
7. Clive Calver, *Thinking Clearly About the Truth* (Monarch)
8. Carl Henry, quoted in *Reaching This Generation*, Brainstormers training video, 1994
9. Lesslie Newbigin, interviewed in YFC vision document 1993
10. J. Richard Middleton and Brian J. Walsh, *Truth Is Stranger Than It Used to Be* (SPCK)
11. Dave Tomlinson, *The Post-Evangelical* (Triangle Books, 1995), p.88
12. Gavin Reid, *The Gagging of God* (IVP, 1969)
13. Charles Pickstone in *The Times*, 24 June 1996
14. This is the philosophy of the Damaris Project, which aims to help Christian leaders to unmask the gods of this world
15. For further work of Brian McLaren see www.emergent.org
16. Thom Hopler, *A World of Difference* (IVP, 1981), p.136

camp — accomplished more in a march of about three.

10

Discipleship Essentials

The spirit of our age makes evangelism easier, but discipleship more difficult.

In Chapter 2, we saw that Christian discipleship has been seriously undermined by our culture's values. In particular:

- rational faith
- feeling faith
- private faith
- material faith.

This chapter looks at how the experiences of youth workers trying to disciple young people can help the wider church with some of these issues.

Incarnational-style discipleship

Very quickly after getting involved in youth ministry, I began to see that the only way to deal with peer pressure was to fight fire with fire.

I had noticed that my residential work with young people – be it over a weekend house party or a summer camp – accomplished more in a matter of hours than three months of the normal youth programme. There was something of real lasting worth and value from these ventures that went far beyond the 'high' of simply being away together. They proved to be fast tracks in Christian growth and maturity.

As I reflected on this, I began to see that adolescent relationships are so all-encompassing and self-defining that for a young person to have any real chance of being discipled, the youth group had to be so good that it became the dominant peer group, the teenager's main anchor and reference point outside of the family. In practice, that is what happened on our residential trips, and it was this sense of community that we tried to replicate on a day-by-day, week-by-week basis. This had obvious dangers of cliquishness which we tried to guard against, but that understanding of the youth group as the alternative peer group was the model which we tried to develop.

As I was looking for a biblical model for what we ought to do, it became apparent that Christianity is better caught than taught. The discipling models that we are given in Scripture appear to suggest that Christian growth and maturity are the results of long-term relational invest-ments. Moses and Joshua, Elijah and Elisha, Eli and Samuel, Paul and Timothy and, of course, Jesus and the disciples all have these traits. So much so that the gospel of Mark sums up the disciples' initial calling as simply 'to be with him' (Mk. 3:14). Truth, it seems, is more power-ful modelled across a dining table than taught across a classroom.

Of course, this whole principle is encapsulated in the incarnation. God became man and crossed the cosmic cultural barrier, not just to tell us the truth, but to be the truth. Jesus met people where they were in a way they understood – a walking, living example of a life that brings God pleasure.

The apostle Paul took this incarnational principle of Christianity very seriously in his church planting. Though he wrote many detailed letters teaching theology and correcting misunderstandings, he earthed all this teaching in the roots of relationship, even to churches he had not as yet met. But to those he had met, he took the incarnational principle even further: 'We loved you so much that we were delighted to share with you not only the gospel of God but our lives as well, because you had become so dear to us' (1 Thes. 2:8); 'Whatever you have learned or received or heard from me, or seen in me – put it into practice. And the God of peace will be with you' (Phil. 4:9); 'Follow my example, as I follow the example of Christ' (1 Cor. 11:1).

What incredible statements. Paul was not, however, an egomaniac. He was very well aware of his own failings (Rom. 7:14–20) and compared with Christ he was but a poor reflection of God's purposes. Neither does Paul ever go as far as to say that he *became* Jesus to people. That goes beyond the teaching of the New Testament. Paul talks of *following* Christ, never *being* Christ. We cannot be Jesus to people (for Jesus is at the right hand of the Father). We can only be an example of what following Christ means. Nevertheless, Paul understood the significance of incarnation; he understood the significance of learning by example. Ultimately he knew that truth comes in lives, not on paper.

It seems that the temptation throughout church history has been to attempt to short cut this process, to break down the sanctification into component parts and try to substitute a lack of relationship with books, conferences and sermons. By and large, it has not worked. As C.S. Lewis put it, 'The longest way round is (still) the shortest way home.'

Such a view turned my ideas about youth work upside

down. A youth worker became someone who entered into the world of a teenager and made Jesus real by the way they lived. Our official role or activity in the youth programme was no more than a starting point for the real work. Programmes and events were only justified if they created an environment where quality relationships could be established. Supremely it meant that it was not so much what we said but who we were that communicated Christ.

If this model of youth work was to happen, the only way was to lead by example. From then on, youth ministry ceased to be a job and became my life. My primary task was to share my life with young people. Later my wife and I were to buy a house with another member of the youth leadership team, simply so that we could operate in this lifestyle pattern more effectively and be more available and geographically closer to the teenagers with whom we were working.

Incarnational-style discipleship and the wider church

In today's church experience, there is much of value that we can learn from youth workers as they explore an incarnational style of ministry.

Fellowship

We have already seen in previous chapters how many feel isolated and lost in today's world and are looking for a sense of 'connectedness'. Sadly, when they encounter the church young people so often find it a mirror image of the very thing they want to get away from – the impersonal institution. In a high-tech society, people are looking for a high-touch church that provides a sense of belonging in a world where they feel lost. In simple terms, friendship is the vehicle of God's love.

THE HEAVY BIT

'The search for community is a quest for values to heal a fragmented humanity. In leadership, hierarchies are being flattened, the corporation style church which we are cloning cannot birth this transformational vision because they have no investment in context or place. We are looking for community. It is a new wineskin. The bottom line is that people want to belong, they want to deal with this unconnectedness.'[1]

Take the way many churches still have home groups, for example. When we are organised into groups and told to have fellowship, do we really expect this to produce the connectedness that people feel they need today? Isn't it more the biblical model that fellowship is more a byproduct of working together than a product of focused efforts? Paul's list of personal greetings in Romans 16 is a classic example of this – lasting friendships forged in the heat of mission.

Providing genuine fellowship for people is one of the biggest areas of tension for a modern church in a postmodern world. Perhaps it is more appropriate to see fellowship as a consequence of mission activity together, rather than something which should be targeted and sought after in its own right.

Accountable leadership

One of the challenging aspects of incarnational-style ministry is the extent to which leaders have to be open and real. Because I wanted to develop a sense of mutual accountability and openness, I invited the group of teenagers to ask me how I was doing with God, as well as me

THE BOTTOM LINE IS THAT PEOPLE WANT TO BELONG ...

asking them. There were times when they needed reminding and times when it was difficult to know quite what to say, but by and large it was a very helpful experience for the young people concerned. It seemed to lead to a healthy atmosphere of openness and accountability among the group, where people genuinely started taking responsibility for each other. Obviously there are weaknesses it would be inappropriate to share, but I have come to see that this mutual openness and accountability is a vital part of the discipling process. How else did the disciples know the anguished content of the Gethsemane prayer unless at a later date Jesus had chosen to tell them? No doubt, years later when they faced horrible deaths, it was a real encouragement to them that the Lord himself had been fearful too and that to be frightened was not a lack of faith or sinful. In this way, Jesus gives us an example of sharing appropriate needs for the strengthening of others.

So often I have listened to the tortured confessions of guilt from teenagers and begun my response very deliberately with, 'Yes, I struggle with that too.' Many times I have seen that simple phrase bring relief to someone's face, take weight off their shoulders and begin a process of forgiveness and healing for their soul.

'It's not that we aren't where we should be, it's that we are not what we should be where we are.'[2]

Incarnation in the culture

I found that because of this understanding that we were entering into their world, and not they into ours, an incarnational-style view of youth ministry brought with it an exciting prospect of trying to disciple people in their own culture.

This was comparatively easy for the kids of Christian families. For them, youth culture was really only a veneer – genuine enough, but in reality only skin deep. They shared in the looks, but by and large not the values, of the world of their peers. They were still teenagers, of course, and therefore wanted to be perceived as different, but deep down their roots were largely the same as mine. In most cases, their parents had seen to it that society's influence had not gone too far beyond fashion styles, music and vegetarianism! A truly biblical, contextualised discipleship programme for these teenagers meant little more than quoting from chart songs, using video clips, keeping talks short and fast moving, and playing lots of games!

It was among the young people from non-Christian homes or even homes hostile to the Christian faith that the challenge of discipling within their culture was enormous. Even for the ones whose parents were sceptical and viewed this period of their lives as 'just a phase they are going through' it was tricky enough. Putting myself in their shoes was very hard. I constantly had to start further back if the gospel was to make sense. But to communicate with those who had been abused, were using drugs, were promiscuous, were illiterate, came from bad homes or were involved in crime was very hard indeed. It was something, I confess, I never really came to terms with.

James, the friend I spoke of in the preface and Chapter 3, was again my doorway to understanding here. For someone dressed as he was, with his very limited reading and writing ability, church was even more intimidating and alien than school. On the occasions when he did come, he just hated it. I soon realised that going to church was positively unhelpful in introducing James to Jesus.

So we set up a small group at our flat for him and his friends, and I tried to spend time with him and his family. James and I played sport together and he learned to swim. I used to try and help him on his paper round when I could and he helped me out on more than one occasion with housework or shopping. He was chosen to play rugby for his school once, and it was the most important appointment of the year for me. It was just about the only success of his entire school career and I would not have missed it for the world.

In those early days of our relationship I felt that I had to challenge much of his lifestyle and behaviour, because it was so chaotic and destructive. Pretty soon I found that all that did was put up barriers between us. After

a while issues like smoking, language, diet, lifestyle,
homework and budgeting all became issues which, while
I consciously tried to model an alternative, I chose not to
speak about with him as they would only get in the way
of what really mattered. I was learning that Jesus works
from the inside out, not the outside in.

The greatest practical problem, and the biggest obstacle
in our relationship, was our understanding of time. I was
part of a large church, with many responsibilities including other staff, and everything revolved around my diary.
James didn't have a diary. He didn't 'book in' anything.
He lived his life on the spur of the moment.

Ever wary of dependency, I made sure that while our
relationship remained strong, we did things together
with other teenagers, as well as involving and introducing him to other friends in the church (something which
incidentally he greatly appreciated, commenting on more
than one occasion that he had made more friends since
he had met me).

Over the years we went through a great deal together.
There were the different stages of adolescence of course
(including a period when he would not come round for
a meal until it was dark, in case people thought he was
babyish). He came on holiday with us and on one occasion
we took him to Spring Harvest, where he spent the whole
week staring at the sea (he had never seen it before). On
his fourteenth birthday we threw a surprise party with
all his mates. When we brought out the cake and candles,
his eyes filled with tears – something I had never seen
before. He explained afterwards that he had never had a
birthday cake.

During this time, faith was naturally part of our relationship. I am sure he eventually understood the gospel,
despite my inability to tell the simple story (looking back I
always used to complicate it). We certainly saw our prayers

answered – mainly when he was in trouble. At times he was bitter about his life and refused to help himself, but most of the time he was a cheerful, fun-loving lad, who just wanted to belong somewhere.

It was in his last year of school that things went badly wrong. One lad followed him around all day, insulting him for the clothes he wore. The last lesson of the day was woodwork, and still the taunts came. James snapped. He picked up a piece of wood and hit the boy with it. As a result he was permanently excluded from school.

I tried very hard to get him back into school. I tried to get him home tuition. I tried to find him an apprenticeship, but there was nothing available. Home all day when his friends were at school, he began to get involved with a group of travellers. James found a sense of belonging, and in less than a year he left home for life on the road.

Now when we occasionally meet it is at the pub. (Though not one of his regular haunts, because, as he explained to me once, 'If we had bother, a "soft life" like you would be no good to me.') His life is full of trouble, prejudice and restlessness, yet this only seems to deepen the camaraderie with his fellow travellers. We both reminisce over what we went through together and he assures me: 'I still remember what you taught me.' But he simply leaves it at that. At the end of the evening he goes back to his world and I go back to mine.

Through the heartbreak of it all, however, some things began to become clear to me. So much of what happened at the church over the ten years I was there was exciting and good. We saw many youngsters come to faith and go on to be disciples. A good number of those who were not from Christian homes are still walking with Jesus and some are doing amazing things for God around the world.

But there were a number of young people, of whom James was one, who just did not fit into the church youth group model. They were so different that they needed an entirely different approach.

Looking back, we failed to disciple them in their culture. If I had the chance again, I think I would have released some of my best youth workers from all church responsibilities and encouraged them to work in a detached way on the street with young people like James.[3]

At the end of the day, what James was longing for was love and acceptance – somewhere he could feel at home and be secure. While he enjoyed good levels of friendship with myself and a few others, he never felt part of the church community. An organised, structured church could never provide that for a young person like James. I mourn the loss of James to the church, but the whole experience made me realise that to truly disciple people in their culture requires flexible models for doing and being God's church.

It is at this crucial point of incarnational leadership that youth work is at its most prophetic to the wider church. When our attempts at Christian discipleship are so often undermined by our culture's hidden values, incarnational leadership can bring real understanding and a realigning to biblical truth, by challenging our assumptions about church.

Rational and feeling faith

There is, of course, no complete answer to the rationalising and emotionalising of faith. To suggest otherwise would be foolishness. However, working with young people does undoubtedly help point towards at least some of the answers.

First, because we are working from the perspective of affirming what is good and challenging what is wrong in youth culture, it means that young people in our churches should be growing up from the start very much more aware than previous generations of the cultural specs they are wearing. This has to be the biggest and most fundamental issue. The reason the rationalising and emotionalising of faith has been such a powerful influence is that most Christians are unaware they even have a set of cultural specs in the first place, and are even less conscious that this colours their understanding and experience of faith. A constructive view of culture leads to people being more aware of the culture of which they are part.

Secondly, because the youth work model is incarnational in its approach, it is by definition people-centred. In a postmodern society, where elements of both rationalism and emotionalism are commonly found, much has to do with the individual's temperament and disposition. Some are by nature more objective, others more emotional. In a people-centred approach to discipleship, there is more chance of personality bias being picked up and addressed. It also takes seriously the idea that Christianity is better caught than taught and has the chance to be modelled more appropriately by the youth leaders themselves.

Private faith

Once we understood that Christian youth leadership meant entering into the world of a teenager and making Jesus real, we set about our research. We soon discovered that a teenager's world revolved around school and family. From this time on, these were our entry points into explaining what it meant to be a Christian. What do you do when mum and dad are arguing? How do you cope when your little brother annoys you? What do you do when you are bullied; when you can't do your homework;

when you don't get into the school team? These issues became the essential entry points for learning to think in a Christian way, applying biblical principles to everyday situations.

We were discovering by accident that incarnational leadership naturally leads to culturally relevant discipleship and that in turn culturally relevant discipleship naturally leads to a more public and robust view of faith. What do I do when my friend is being bullied? What do I say to my friends when they are trying pot? What do I do when my friends are having casual sex? Take the principle of discipling in someone's natural culture seriously and faith will struggle to remain private. Perhaps one reason faith has in so many cases become privately engaging but publicly irrelevant is that our induction into it has not been biblically incarnational, so faith is removed from the real world.

Putting it succinctly, incarnation leads to contextualisation, which leads to relevance in the public world.

Exposing dualism

It was on this journey to publicly relevant faith that questions were raised by some older Christians about a programme that included subjects such as 'Bringing up your parents', 'Ultimate sex' and 'Does saint mean swot?' Through subsequent conversations I first came to understand a major theological problem facing the church that previously I had only read about. Lurking behind their unease that these subjects were too worldly was a very shadowy customer indeed – dualism. Ultimately it was understanding dualism that explained to me why evangelicals have had such a difficult time with the issue of culture.

Careful dualism

Dualism itself should not be a dirty word. It basically means 'when two subjects cannot be reduced into one'. So there are areas of the Christian faith where careful dualism needs to be affirmed. Take God and creation, for example. We do not believe that a mountain or a river is God to be worshipped. God made the world, but is distinct from it. Anything less and our worship becomes confused. Paul upholds another important dualism in Romans 6–8 when he contrasts the work of the sinful nature and the Spirit.

Careless dualism

Trouble arises when careful dualism becomes careless dualism; when biblical dualism becomes cultural dualism; when a simplistic mind-set of two worlds, the physical and the spiritual, becomes the filter through which we read the Bible and see all of life itself. Everything then has to be either ruled in or out, of God or of the world, sacred or secular. Such a black-and-white universe does not exist and owes more to Plato than it does to Christ, but its enduring attraction is that it makes life so much simpler.

Simple it might be, but harmless it is not! Thriving on half-truths and a basic human desire to have everything neatly labelled, careless dualism left unchallenged can completely undermine Christianity's role in the world, because it whispers to us all the time that we should not really be there.

Dualism's double whammy

Dualism's sinister power is that it is so deeply embedded in both our non-Christian worldview and our traditional church thinking that we never notice how it colours our vision. Our non-Christian specs are distorting enough, but tint them with the misguided thought of the church and dualism becomes a double whammy that catches out most of us at one time or another. Let us look at this double whammy in more detail.

Dualism in the Western world today

Since the Enlightenment, a false divide in the Western world between faith and reason has dominated the way we think.

The Enlightenment 'for all its real light' (as Newbigin so wonderfully puts it) over-emphasised human reason so much that in the end anything that could not be objectively examined was not accepted as true. Faith was held to be outside this realm of testing, so a false dualism took hold. Faith was no longer a way to discovering truth.

This climate of 'unreasonable reason' pressured many churches to take sides – either emphasising thinking at the expense of experience, or emphasising experience at the expense of common sense. Meanwhile, for the vast majority of people in the Western world the perception was simply that the men in white coats and the men in dog collars had got into a scrap and the men in white coats had won. Science was now fact, and religion was speculation.

Dualism in the church today

As if dualism in the world were not enough to cause us problems, at the same time dualism has strong roots in the church. It was particularly after the conversion of Emperor Constantine that dualism became a problem. Suddenly at peace with the state after years of persecution, the church quickly found itself caught up in supporting the government instead of holding to its prophetic and evangelistic calling.

Many committed Christians, frustrated by this 'worldly compromise', came out to start alternative churches and in doing so over-emphasised the 'come out and be separate' nature of true faith. From then on, it would appear that the more devout the movement, the more dualistic its disciples. They had a clear upstairs/downstairs worldview, where things were either of the flesh or of the spirit, and there was an emphasis on abstaining from worldly pleasures and pursuing a higher, less compromised spiritual life. Ironically, far from being 'in the world but not of it' they became 'of the world and not in it', all because of dualism. In many ways today we still live with this legacy of thought.

A CASE OF CARELESS DUALISM...

'I cannot believe that a person who has ever known the love of God can relish a secular novel. Let me visit your chamber, your parlour, or wherever you keep your books. What is here? Byron, Scott, Shakespeare and a host of triflers and blasphemers of God.'[4]

A biblical response to dualism

All this is somewhat ironic, given that the Bible writers went out of their way to challenge careless dualism.

John's gospel, for example, was written to explain

the Christian message to Greeks seeped in a dualistic philosophy. With that audience, he deliberately chose to use the word 'logos' to describe Jesus. The logos was part of the sacred world to the Greeks, so the opening words of the book struck a genuine chord of familiarity with them: 'In the beginning was the Word, and the Word was with God, and the Word was God. He was with God in the beginning' (Jn. 1:1–2).

No sooner had common ground been established, however, than John started pushing the boundaries of his readers' understanding: 'He was in the world' (v.10), and then sending shock waves through the system with: 'The Word became flesh' (v.14). Four carefully chosen words which for all time stamped Christianity's refusal to fit into a dualistic understanding of the universe.

The apostle Paul, likewise, set about challenging this underlying two-world assumption of many of his readership:

'See to it that no-one takes you captive through hollow and deceptive philosophy, which depends on human tradition and the basic principles of this world rather than on Christ.' (Col. 2:8)

'Since you died with Christ to the basic principles of this world, why, as though you still belonged to it, do you submit to its rules: "Do not handle! Do not taste! Do not touch!"? These are all destined to perish with use, because they are based on human commands and teachings. Such regulations indeed have an appearance of wisdom, with their self-imposed worship, their false humility and their harsh treatment of the body, but they lack any value in restraining sensual indulgence… .' 'Whatever you do, work at it with all your heart, as working for the Lord, not for

men, since you know that you will receive an inheritance
from the Lord as a reward. It is the Lord Christ you are
serving.' (Col. 2:20–23; 3:23–24)

Paul seems to treat dualism not as a question of either/or,
but of both/and. Everything in creation was made good
(1 Tim. 4:4), but it has also been marred by sin and so is
fallen and bad (2 Cor. 6:14–18, 7:1; Rom. 3:23). However,
through Christ, God has acted to rescue the world and
reconcile it to himself (2 Cor. 5:19). Jesus himself referred
to this tension of a fallen and yet created humanity in his
phrase 'You, though you are evil, know how to give good
gifts to your children' (Mt. 7:11). For the Christian, then,
careless dualism is not an option; rather the Bible calls us
to live holding in tension this fallen and yet God-created
world order.

C.S. Lewis sums up the Bible's refusal to slip into dualism and yet not dismiss it out of hand quite wonderfully:
'There is no neutral ground in the universe. Every square
inch, every split second, is claimed by God and counter-
claimed by Satan.'[5]

Dualism through church history

Fortunately there have been a number of thinking
Christians through the centuries, alert to the dangers of
casual dualism. In his excellent book on fashion[6], Mike
Starkey notes how Calvin, despite the fact that many of
his followers were to become world denyers, offered a
positive framework for understanding the material world,
describing it even as a 'theatre of glory'.

For the Puritans there was not the war between the
spiritual and material that their reputation for piety
suggests. They had 'a hearty earthiness, based on the

understanding that in the routine, practical tasks of daily life, were the arenas where we meet God'.[7]

Others, too, have eloquently and powerfully spoken against casual dualism.

When Paul says 'come out and be separate' he does not mean that Christians ought to take no interest in anything on earth except religion. To neglect science, art, literature and politics – to read nothing which is not directly spiritual – to know nothing about what is going on among mankind and never to look at a newspaper – to care nothing about the government of one's own country and to be utterly indifferent to the persons who guide its councils and make its laws – all this may seem very right and proper in the eyes of some people. But I take leave to think that it is an idle, selfish neglect of duty.[8]

'When the church ceases to be concerned with the world then it ceases to hear God speak to it. For God's conversation with the church is a conversation about the world and the church must be willing to converse about the world if it is to converse with God. It is the world which is the direct object of God's action. He made it, He loved it, He saved it, He will judge it through Jesus Christ. Indeed, a church that is disobedient to its commission to go to the world becomes a menace to the world itself.'[9]

Dualism today

The trouble is that a biblical worldview is far more difficult to hold to than a careless dualistic one. Dualism is neatly labelled, whereas a more biblical worldview requires us to live with paradox and tension.

Chris Seaton, in his helpful book *Your Mind Matters*, highlights six areas (all beginning with E) where careless dualism still holds sway in Christian thinking today.

Ethics

Careless dualism leads to an unbalanced Christian ethic, where we are strong on private morality, but weak on public truth. As a consequence, we are far more comfortable talking about personal issues like abortion and pornography than public ones like education and employment; global trade and poverty.

Evangelism

When the only thing that we can say about the world is that it is utterly fallen, going into it (Mt. 28) becomes more a question of ingrab rather than outreach – rescuing individuals into the church rather than seeing the church changing society.

Ecology

If the world is only fallen, then it is doomed to destruction anyway, and the environment is not a priority for Christians. After all, we are about saving souls, not whales!

Eschatology

An over-emphasis on a fallen world can easily lead to a preoccupation with future things like the Second Coming of Christ and revival. If we are not very careful, this becomes a serious cop-out, a head-in-the-sand mentality of 'Jesus is going to come back one day and will make everything right, so just sit tight' rather than the biblical 'thy kingdom come, thy will be done on earth, as it is in heaven'. To pray for revival and/or for Christ to come again, without doing anything about it, is actually a form of escapism.

Employment

Our upstairs/downstairs legacy of life leads to honouring so-called full-time Christian workers at the expense of recognising that all Christians are full time by definition of being Christian.

Engagement

If our cultural spectacles colour the world as only fallen, then rather than seeing the arts as humanity's inherited creativeness from God we'll be seeing the arts as frivolous entertainment to be avoided by Christians. The cinema is not called the 'sin-ema' for nothing.

Ultimately, careless dualism reduces Christians to a state of spiritual schizophrenia – seeking a label for everything rather than living with tension in a world caught between the now and the not yet. Howard Snyder sees dualism's influence in the church today as primarily affecting our focus of attention. If we succumb to careless dualism, we focus on the church in the world, whereas those living with a more biblical worldview tend to focus on the kingdom of God instead. He put it like this: 'Church people think about how to get people into the church, kingdom people think about how to get the church into the kingdom. Church people worry that the world might change the church, kingdom people work to see the church change the world.'[10]

This was exactly the issue we faced in the youth programme. Incarnational-style discipleship had led to a robust, publicly relevant faith that focused young Christians on changing their world. Older Christians, without that incarnational understanding, had a more 'private' faith and, as a result, were much more concerned about the danger of the world polluting the church.[11]

Material faith

When every aspect of life is understood to be God's, Western materialism inevitably comes under his spotlight.

Following a youth weekend away, in which we had highlighted the appalling needs of the two-thirds world and compared it with the wealth and affluence of the West, the youth group really took up the challenge of becoming world Christians. Thanks to the input of a team from the Salvation Army led by Phil Wall, they coined the phrase the MAD Team (Make A Difference).

They started with themselves. I watched them form small accountability groups where they would confess their sins to each other and ask each other to take responsibility in prayer and advice for the way they handled their sexuality and their money. I watched them start sharing clothes and resources so that they could give the money they would have otherwise spent to third world related issues. It was fantastic to see.

Then came one of the most enjoyable moments of my ten years of youth ministry. A group of young people came round for coffee. They had just spent three hours blitzing a house (cleaning it from top to bottom) so it was fit for an old man to return to after a period in hospital. This was something that Jez, a sixteen-year-old lad in the group, had arranged completely on his own. There was not an adult in sight and none of the youth team had even known that it was taking place. The group had, by themselves, decided that this was something Christians ought to be doing and had simply got on with the job. By all accounts (and as you would expect they were pretty graphic) the house had been in a terrible state with human and animal faeces in several rooms, and they had to buy treble the quantity of disinfectant that they had anticipated. Nevertheless, the young people eventually got the place clean so that the man could return from hospital. Jez was the hero that night. Not only had he organised the whole thing, but he had led by example and volunteered to do the toilet himself. As I heard them laughing and talking that evening and sensing among them a feeling of accomplishment, I was very proud to be part of what God was doing in that group.

Then came the awkward bit. They started asking questions about what they could actually do in terms of direct action to improve the lot of people in the two-thirds world. As I tried to explain that it wasn't as simple as it first appeared, I was met with a barrage of 'why nots'. I was forced to admit that my culturally conditioned cynicism was further from the biblical text than their simple idealism and as we worked through the issues together, idealism and realism met in an understanding that we could not solve everything, but we could do something. We could make a difference. So the Ethiopian MAD Project was born.

Over the next few years it was to result in twice taking groups of young people out to the slums of Addis Ababa, to experience first hand the squalor and degradation of some of the worst slum areas in Africa. While we did some work out there and tried to encourage people as best we could, the main purpose of our visits was to make a video to use for fundraising once we returned.

As the young people prepared to go out, worked hard to raise their air fares, spoke of the traumas of the visit upon their return and were brave enough to lead whole school assemblies as well as teach lessons about their experiences, many adults in the church shared with me how challenged they were personally by the courage and boldness of the young people concerned. Some were challenged to give sacrificially. Two adults even gave up their normal jobs to live out more directly the priorities we were all learning about. Over time, the whole of the church was galvanised into action for the sake of the marginalised in our world. The MAD Project soon ceased to be simply a youth project

HAVING HAS REPLACED BEING...

and encompassed the whole of the church family. To date the church has raised in excess of £25,000 towards the work of the Christians in the slums.

When many of our churches today are held back in witness of the gospel simply because of the grip materialism has on our lives – when our understanding of the nature of God's love is compromised by our insistence on dividing evangelism and social action as if we can cut and paste with God's character – perhaps it is time to sit at the feet of those who maybe don't see the multinationals and the trade deficits as the giants we do, but armed with little more than some biblical principles and youthful idealism, go off to fight for justice.

After ten years of working with young people, I am convinced that we dismiss their youthful idealism at our peril. We have much to listen to and learn from.

THE HEAVY BIT

'Having has replaced being... Want becomes need. Consumption is the source of meaning. To hide it we have adopted a language of convenience again. We don't talk about debt and the damage we are doing to future generations. What do we call it? We call it credit. Credit cards are a status symbol. We treat debt as credit as if it is good.'

Summary of Chapter 10

Working with young people in their peer groups forces us to take the incarnational style of biblical discipleship seriously. That means that we learn to enter their world, not insist that they enter ours.

This not only helps Christians grow up more aware of culture's influence on their lives, but also encourages a more public and robust attitude to their faith, which in turn exposes the careless dualistic thinking so prevalent in the church.

In short, incarnational-style discipleship is the single biggest factor in helping the church out of its culture trap.

NOTES

1. Phillips and Okholm, *Christian Apologetics in a Post-Modern World* (IVP)
2. Os Guinness, *The Gravedigger File* (Hodder & Stoughton, 1983), p.82
3. Mike Breen, *Outside In* (Scripture Union, 1993), Bob Mayo, *Gospel Exploded* (Triangle Books, 1996), Pete Ward, *Youth Culture and the Gospel* (Marshall Pickering, 1992) have all documented this model of youth work.
4. Charles Finney quoted in Hofstadter, *Anti-intellectualism in American Life*, quoted in Os Guinness, *Fit Bodies, Fat Minds* (Hodder & Stoughton, 1995), p.64
5. C. S. Lewis, 'Peace Proposals for Brother Every and Mr Bethel' in Walter and Hooper (eds), *Christian Reflections* (Fount Paperbacks, 1981), p.52
6. Mike Starkey, *Fashion and Style* (Monarch, 1995), p.57
7. J. C. Ryle, *Worldly Conformity* (1878), quoted by Os Guinness, *Fit Bodies, Fat Minds* (Hodder & Stoughton, 1995), p.65
8. D.T. Niles, *A Treasury of Great Preaching* (Word, 1971), Vol. 12, p.188
9. Howard Snyder, *Liberating the Church* (Marshall Pickering, 1983), quoted by Chris Seaton, *Your Mind Matters* (Word Books, 1993), p.68
10. 'Religion is a full blooded experience which includes all the receptors – all the senses with the rational mind being only one locus of information about reality... . New paradigm Christians see no reason why they should exclude visions and ecstatic experiences from the realm of religious knowledge.' Donald Miller, *Reinventing American Protestantism* (University of California Press, 1997) quoted in *Mission as Transformation* Ed Samuel and Sugden (Regum books, 1999) p.18 preface
11. Roy McCloughry, *Tomorrow's World* (Christian Institute Lectures, 1996)

11

Educational Essentials

He who learns from one occupied in learning drinks from a
running stream. He who learns from one who has learned
all he has to teach, drinks the green mantle of the standing
pool.[1]

You can't work with young people for very long without
recognising that school is second only to family in its
life-shaping influence upon young people. For any church
giving priority to work with teenagers, school therefore
has to become an important area of their involvement.
And once this happens, there are things for the church
to learn.

School – a doorway to the wider community

Schools are products of their communities. All the strengths
and weaknesses of a particular area are reflected in a
school. If an area is economically depressed, for example,
then that lack of finance is inevitably going to be seen in
the standard of school uniforms, the availability of money
for sports equipment and the level of financial support
that the PTA can provide. If an area is multicultural, so
will the school be, and if an area is violent then the school

will not be immune from that problem either. In short, schools are micro-communities, mirror images of the areas from which they draw their pupils.

This means that schools can provide a number of benefits to any church taking its input into school life seriously. The first and most obvious: get to know your school and you get to know your community. Schools can be a tremendous help in first getting to grips with an area. As I became more involved with my local school, I realised that it acted as a magnet, an access point for many statutory and business organisations. My first contact with adult education, sports clubs, counsellors, local businesses and police, for example, all came through meetings at school.

If we take on board this idea that school is a mirror image of the wider community, its make-up and attitudes, the church has a lot more to learn as it reflects on the nature of its relationship with school.

Plausibility versus credibility

I well remember my first approach to the local school to see if I could take an assembly. I had only been a youth minister for three months and I was keen to stress my commitment to the educational process and to distance myself from any view that saw church in school as a means of proselytising. Unknown to me, though, a few years previously the school had been hit by an irresponsible evangelist who had been very insensitive in a school assembly, with fairly dire consequences. As a result, years later, the head teacher was extremely guarded and non-committal with me. It eventually took a reference from another school before I had the chance to do even an assembly.

Having survived this first hurdle, however, I was invited again, and within a year or two I was a regular visitor to the school, teaching lessons, taking assemblies and involved in the school pastoral care system, as well as lunchtime clubs. One development followed another as the level of trust and relationship deepened. Slowly, what was happening was that the perception of the church held by the senior staff was being changed. We were now being seen as fellow community providers. In effect, our schools work was winning back lost ground in post-Christian Britain.

Looking back now, this level of trust and involvement that the church established with the local school was crucial to the success of a number of projects. Our schools work established a level of community credibility and trust which could not have been achieved any other way. Parents tended to take their lead from the school. If the school was prepared to trust us with their pupils, then so would the parents.

Once again, the youth worker's experience in school has a lot to teach the wider church about (mis)communication between God's people and society. When I first met the head teacher I was concerned only about the credibility of the Christian message in the educational setting. However, what interested them was not the credibility of what I would say but the plausibility of who I was. Churches often approach evangelism as if the credibility of our beliefs is all that counts. As my first contact with the school shows, however, it is not the credibility of the message but the plausibility of who we are that is the main issue. This can only be overcome by building relationships over time.

Evangelism and education

I had always been taught that to evangelise directly was an abuse of the educational context. It was the job of schools to educate, the job of churches to evangelise. But as I taught a multifaith syllabus and as I taught life's ultimate issues, I discovered that good education is evangelistic. As I encouraged pupils to think deeply about their lives and evaluate the different belief systems for themselves, and to think about life's ultimate questions, the process was by definition evangelistic in that it naturally led people to search for truth and so took them steps closer to Christ. It totally legitimately allowed the claims of Christ to be critically examined and weighed up against other religious views.

Here lies another exciting insight into evangelistic work in the current cultural setting. If good education is evangelistic, the church ought to consider running adult education classes at local colleges and schools, helping people to think through life's ultimate issues. Or how about parenting courses for our communities – practically orientated, but with enough about love, forgiveness and identity to set people thinking about the bigger issues? Here, perhaps, are some of the pioneer paths for evangelism as we embark on a new millennium.

CU or lessons?

One of the more revealing insights from my involvement with school, though, came as the constraints on my time forced me to set priorities. I could either give precedence to supporting the small number of Christians who met at lunchtime in the school Christian Union, or I could, through continuing my lesson input, work with a larger number of young people not in any way connected with the church. Reasoning that the Christian teenagers had churches to support them and without fully appreciating the significance of the decision I was making, I chose the latter.

It was very interesting how this move was perceived among some of my Christian friends in the church. Supporting church kids at the school's Christian Union was viewed as a legitimate Christian ministry. Teaching RE was not. Once again I was encountering the careless dualism that hides behind so much Christian thought.

School is where it counts

I am often asked what has been the highlight of my years in youth ministry. Without doubt, one of the best moments was a phone call at the end of a summer term from a form teacher I barely knew. 'I want to thank you for my best year in teaching so far,' she said. I was bewildered because I had never even taught her group. 'My form class this year has had five young people who have started attending your church. I have watched their lives change and in turn witnessed the atmosphere of the whole tutor group change. It has been a most wonderful year.'

There have been many great moments over ten years of youth ministry, with memorable weekends away, times when God's presence was tangible in meetings, the joy of seeing young people converted and great projects come to fulfilment. However, that phone call still stands out as one of the best moments of all. Ultimately, Christian ministry has to be measured by the salt-and-light effect that Christians have in their world: 'By their fruits you shall know them.'

Learning to teach

It is not only in our interaction with school life that the church has things to learn. We have so much to benefit from in thinking through the educational process itself.

One of the greatest challenges facing all youth workers is how to teach God's word to young people. Just how do we encourage 'the word of God to dwell in you richly' (Col. 3:16) in a mixed age and mixed ability group of children who are, in the main, not that keen on more education?

Neither do we have the opportunity to teach them for very long. We normally do not have more than four years before young people move away to further education or out to work. In reality, it is a very small window of opportunity.

'It is a good thing that separation must come, otherwise that inner strength that is the purpose of education will not be strengthened.'[2]

Faced with these challenges as a youth worker, I sought to clarify in my mind the priorities for balanced biblical teaching. I was soon to realise that thinking about good education brings principles that are as valuable in the house group and the pulpit as they are in the youth group.

Good old Tim

As we turned the corner, she was lying on the path in obvious agony. It was late evening and we were returning from a long walk on yet another church youth weekend away. The youth group rushed to the lady's assistance. She explained that while out jogging she had twisted her ankle and was now incapable of putting any weight on it. A cursory glance showed that her ankle was very swollen, and she would not let anybody touch it.

Little did they know it, but the young people were unwittingly engaged in one of our more creative and valuable 'teaching times'. The lady was acting, the swelling was nothing more than cotton wool and the next five minutes were about to enter group folklore.

While the teenagers were discussing what to do, I said to the lady: 'I'm terribly sorry, but we've paid good money to come on this weekend and if we help you now we will miss our tea. What we'll do is hurry back to the centre and let them know where you are.' (All the youth leaders had been briefed to say nothing and simply follow me as I started to stride away.)

As you can imagine, the young people were somewhat bewildered and not a little indignant. After about twenty paces I turned and with as much authority as I could muster, said: 'Come on, you really must come. It's the best way to help.'

To my horror a large group of the younger ones started to follow – grumbling but nevertheless doing what I said. This was not in my plan, but I was committed now. A few steps further on I turned and insisted that the others follow. At this point the majority of the group, embarrassed and angry (some even apologising to the lady on the ground), started to follow. I was just wondering what I was going to do next when Tim, one of the eldest boys, who had not left the lady's side, shouted in a very loud voice: 'Andy, this is wrong.'

Not a little relieved, I gathered the youth group around the lady and said: 'If you think I have just made a mistake, please stand on my right.' En masse they jumped at the chance to register their disapproval. 'And if you were really prepared to do something about it, stay there.' They became very quiet and thoughtful as the penny dropped and slowly all walked over to my left, except Tim.

'We have spent the whole weekend learning about Christians making a difference in the world for God,' I said. 'If you can't do it here, what hope is there when we get home?' With that, I helped the lady up. It was only as she started to walk that the kids realised that it had all been a set up. I seem to remember I got rather muddy on the way home, but it was worth it. It was a lesson that none of us ever forgot.

Clarify the purpose

My first goal was to equip teenagers with how to think as Christians in a non-Christian world. This is very different from teaching them what they ought to think. True Christian education is teaching people how to think, not what to think. The Bible says that the truth shall set us free, so true Christian thinking should be characterised by openness and questioning, and a humble delight in truth revealed. 'Simplistic legalism never creates mature disciples; rather one of the vital tasks before the contemporary church is to train all of us, but especially our children, to critique and evaluate all around us.'[3]

The problem then arose of actually recognising when people truly knew and understood something they had been taught. Respected educationalist John Holt helps clarify this in his book *How Children Fail*. He argues that to really know something we must be able to:

● state it in our own words
● give examples of it
● recognise it in various circumstances
● see the connection between it and other ideas and facts

- make use of it in various ways
- foresee some of its consequences
- state its opposite or converse.

We know something, he concluded, when we understand why.[4]

Clarify the process
But we make a mistake if we focus exclusively on the style and content of what is being taught.

UNAWARENESS AWARENESS INTEREST

ACCEPTANCE CONVICTION COMMITMENT

When people acquire knowledge they progress through six stages

For example, social acceptance is critical to learning. This is because the single most important issue in learning is the ability to enquire. To enquire requires confidence, and confidence only comes through feeling accepted and comfortable within the group. The learning environment, then, is as important as the teaching content when it comes to education.

Children fail

- when they are afraid
- when they are disappointing or displeasing adults
- when they are bored
- when it is trivial or dull
- when they are confused
- when words or ideas are above them
- when the setting is unstable.

Another educational tool which may be helpful in youth work, as well as to the wider church, is the stepping method. This is a teaching aid designed to cope with a mixed ability group. It provides people with a structure of work (like a worksheet, for example) which gives maximum access to everyone by setting easy tasks to begin with and gradually getting harder, so that people are then free to study up to their appropriate level of ability. Another model is to teach a steady progression of ideas, but using a variety of stimuli to generate thought about the particular subject. Both of these education tools are fairly easily incorporated even into a standard sermon and even more easily into home-group material, etc.

Teaching organically

In his book *The Gospel Exploded*, Bob Mayo documents the ups and downs of trying to teach street teenagers in Bermondsey about Christ.

He was to discover that there was a massive difference

in the way that young people on the street and teenagers in the church were best taught. 'I had been taught that discovering Jesus followed on from understanding Jesus. By contrast, what we began to teach the young people of the street was that understanding follows on from discovery.' Mayo realised that an organic approach was more helpful than an informational approach. In other words, 'Christians pray' is information; 'try talking to God yourself' is organic. 'Christians worship in church' is information; 'come and sing' is organic. By trying to teach prayer and worship, Mayo argues, we only complicate and confuse 'the most natural thing in the world'. Organic knowledge also has the advantage that it is self-feeding rather than being dependent on outside input.

On top of this organic education, Mayo discovered that simple story-telling was the best way forward for young people on the street to grasp the implications of the gospel. He constantly found himself having to resist the temptation to explain, and simply tell the Bible story. This way the Bible became more real and alive to teenagers because they were given the freedom to interpret the story for themselves. Mayo was in effect discovering on the streets of London a principle that many a missionary has discovered before him.

In order for this approach to work, however, it required an environment that was spontaneous and unstructured and that made itself up around what everyone wanted to know. Informal education required an informal setting.

Balanced teaching

I am indebted to Nick Pollard of The Damaris Trust for his incisive thinking about the nature of genuine Christian education.

Didactic versus critical

When debate rages in education about the didactic versus the critical method, Christians have to question whether either of them is an appropriate way of communicating Christian truth.

The traditional didactic method goes back to Plato, where a teacher teaches and the student listens and learns. The critical method, however, is rooted in the Enlightenment, where dogma was replaced by reason. This influenced education to the extent that teachers were now encouraging students to explore and find truth for themselves. The 1967 Plowden Report moved schools towards this latter view.

Both approaches are based on a different view of truth, and both views are inadequate from a Christian perspective. The didactic method tends towards a dogmatic view of truth: I know it and I will tell you about it. The critical method tends towards a relativist view of truth: no one has the monopoly on truth, so let us discover our own truth together. We must build a Christian model of truth, says Pollard, if we are to have truly Christian education.

Christian truth is obviously not relativist, but neither is it didactic. God has not revealed all truth to us and the truth he has revealed is in part hidden by our fallen human minds. There is absolute truth, but it is only God who holds it. So Christian education is God-centred and both teacher and pupil are trying to discover truth together. It starts with the teacher, but it is not dogmatic, and the student critiques and responds, all the while keeping the notion of truth as something to be discovered as we try to love God with our minds.

The perfect teacher

'The visual dominates, the verbal recedes. Images replace words, words and images are pushed into opposition. It is crazy, though. God created them both. The original word and the ultimate image were in total harmony. God intended them to relate. Words inform us through our minds, images affect us through our eyes. Images call for recognition, words provide understanding. Jesus Christ was at once the Word and the Image of the Invisible God. He was the Word and He spoke God's truth and anyone who had seen Him, the Image, had seen the Father. The sight of a man dying was neither self-explanatory, nor left to create its own impression, it needed God's Word to reveal its meaning. Since Word and Image went together in Him, they cannot be opposed. Jesus did many miraculous signs, but without His interpretation their significance was lost'.[5]

There is nothing like being faced with a bunch of stroppy fourteen-year-olds who don't want to learn to make the Christian youth worker ask the question, 'How would Jesus teach this group?'

As we learn about learning from the Gospels, a number of things become apparent about Jesus' teaching style:

● Learning is centred on the learner, not the subject. Jesus communicated truth differently, depending on his audience (see for example Lk. 10:25–37; Mk. 10:17–25).

- Learning seemed to happen in a rhythm of action and reflection. For example, 54 per cent of his recorded encounters were initiated by questions.
- Learning had defined objectives (Mk. 3:13–15).
- It took place in a community and the friction within that community added to the learning dynamic (Lk. 22:24).
- Jesus' teaching often took place in an atmosphere of affirmation and expectancy (Mk. 1:17; Jn. 1:42).
- Jesus' style of teaching was not about the transmission of impersonal fact, but rather the transformation of a person (Mt. 7:24).
- Learning was inseparably related to everyday life (e.g. Mt. 10:29; 11:3; 12:10).
- Learning was aided by enforcement and repetition (Mk. 8:29–33). The hardest lessons, it seems, need to be repeated.
- Jesus told stories. There are sixty-three parables in the Gospels and only four of them are explained. Jesus trusted the inductive process, in sharp contrast to the Pharisees who were orthodox and deductive. Jesus' stories were the point, their simplicity was their chief charm.
- Jesus asked questions to make people think and involved people practically, that lessons might be reinforced (Mt. 4:19). These practical sessions were followed up with debriefs and retreats for more learning (e.g. Lk. 9, a rhythm of action and reflection).
- Fundamentally, Jesus' style of education takes place through studying a living example (Jn. 13).
- Jesus was an informal teacher. He used opportunities as they arose, especially questions, to take people deeper in their understanding of the kingdom.

In their book *Learning to Preach Like Jesus*, Ralph and Greg Lewis suggest that Jesus' teaching style took account of what we understand today are the functions of the left and right side of the human brain. The left side is analytical and verbal, the right side is instinctive and visual. So the left is labels, the right is images; grammar and vocabulary are left, but poetry comes from the right; the left is rational, but the right is relational. They argue that Jesus switches between the two in his teaching methods and operates a three-level brain of preaching. The stem of the brain is instinctive, the limbic is emotion and feeling, and the cerebrum is the thinking. They argue that we need to preach like Jesus and preach at all three levels of the brain, and that it is best to move from right to left quickly, i.e. every four to five minutes. The test of Jesus' communication and the test for any preachers today, they suggest, is 'and the common people heard him gladly'.

For those with ears to hear, the experience of youth workers involved in the educational process has a lot to say for the benefit of the wider church.

Summary of Chapter 11

Schools are doorways to their local community. How we are involved and perceived there is a valuable learning experience for the church's wider task of being salt and light in society.

But it is in learning about learning that the church has most to benefit through its educational involvement.

While adult congregations are largely passive learners, young people are not. While adult congregations tend to be tolerant of poor teaching, young people are not.

The value of teaching today's young people lies in the severity of the challenge. It forces us to think again about the purpose and process of what we are trying to do and drives us to learn, both from educational theory and supremely from the perfect teacher himself.

The lessons found here are sure to be of benefit to the whole congregation, not just young people.

NOTES

1. A.J. Stott, 1805
2. William Temple quoted by Michael Harper, *Let My People Grow* (Logos International, 1977), p.66
3. Gavin McGrath, *NB Magazine* (UCCF), June/July 1996
4. John Holt, *How Children Fail* (Pelican Books)
5. Extracted and arranged from Gavin McGrath, *NB Magazine* (UCCF), June/July 1996

12

Missionary Essentials (1)

'Christians working among the young therefore face in principle the same issues that any missionary faces when going into another culture; questions of language, custom, attitudes, values and ideas are all put into the melting pot.'[1]

For a number of years, youth workers have been looking to the missionary writers for insights and advice in communicating the gospel across cultures. In fact, 'youth missionary' is becoming an in phrase.

Increasingly, however, there is a widespread understanding that all church leaders, not just youth workers, have to communicate across cultures to be effective. Here lies perhaps the greatest value of youth work to the contemporary church. Youth work trains us to think like missionaries.

Throughout the next two chapters I tend to use 'missionary' as a very general term. Of course, you can't possibly lump several hundred years of history across seven continents of the world with a variety of diverse views and approaches (let alone theologies) under one label, but because there is not the space for a variety of views on each issue I have generalised. The missionary writer Vincent Donovan wrote about his return to the United States after years in Africa:

OUT OF THE FRYING PAN INTO THE YOUTH CLUB...

'I realised that here on the home front, I had left behind me one of the most exotic tribes of all – the young people of America. They have their own form of dress, symbolised by their omnipresent blue jeans; their own food, not always the most nutritious; their own music, which I confess, I do not understand; their own rituals, enacted as they listen to their music in concert; their own language, their own values, remarkably similar from New York to California. Dress, food, music, ritual, language, values – these are the things that make up a tribe, or a sub-culture, as they have been called. It is to that tribe, as they are, that the gospel must be brought.'[2]

Christianity – a threat to culture?

More times than I care to remember as a youth worker what I wanted to say never got heard, simply because who I was and what I had to say were perceived to be a threat to the peer group's way of living.

I will never forget one particular Boys' Brigade summer camp at which I was asked to speak. The first night, despite my best efforts, I could hardly even get their attention. The message to me was clear: they were at camp to have a good laugh, and the evening talk did not fit in with that agenda.

As I went to bed that night I could see that radical measures were called for, so at 1am, without the knowledge of the senior officers, I approached the two oldest lads' tents and enquired if they wanted to join me on a raiding party to the local scout camp. As you can imagine, I wasn't short of volunteers.

It was a long and hilarious night, stories of which were to become legendary and bind the group together for many years to come. Crucially, though, it completely changed the atmosphere of the camp and the lads' interest in Christianity. No longer was the Christian gospel threatening to their culture – it was actually leading the way! The very next evening they were all listening. Illustrations came thick and fast from the night before, and by the end of the week a number had moved on significantly in their relationship with Christ. In missiological terms, the gospel had been heard on its own merits once it was understood that it did not constitute a threat to the culture of the young people concerned.

So much of what is misunderstood and frowned upon by the wider church as 'frivolous' youth work actually is missiologically justifiable. It is part of establishing the gospel without the adult world's trappings. Sadly, though, it is not until you are identifying with youth culture that you can actually see the need for it, and the tragic result is that many youth workers are viewed as unspiritual or shallow (or with just plain bewilderment and misunderstanding) by their congregations, simply because the church has failed to learn from the missionaries. The truth is that the gospel needs to be placed in a context appropriate to someone's culture, and in youth work that often means raw energy and fun. So often it is not the youth worker who is shallow; it is the wider church because it has simply not thought the issue through. The tragic result is many a youth worker senses the same loneliness and isolation that the missionary knows only too well. In seeking to reach a particular group they get caught between two cultures and can find themselves truly at home in neither.

Again the parallels are obvious for the wider church. Christianity's general failure to engage the working class is a case in point. It is well documented that faced with the reading, diary-administered formal relationships and smartly dressed culture of the predominantly middle-class church, working people tend to feel threatened and alienated and so stay away. Ministry groups like those working with travellers or athletes, though, have learned to organise the church experience in culturally appropriate ways and in doing so point the way forward for the whole of the church in the West. We have to learn to bring the good news of Jesus to people without inadvertently threatening their culture.

SO-CALLED 'FRIVOLOUS' YOUTH WORK
IS MISSIOLOGICALLY JUSTIFIABLE...

Drawing the line

When does not threatening a culture unconsciously cross over the line and become a compromise of Christian truth? For those willing to learn, the missionary writers teach us the principle of balance – on the one hand Jesus challenges and reveals sin in every culture, but on the other hand there are aspects of culture which are not incompatible with the lordship of Christ and therefore need not be discarded but rather preserved and transformed.

THE HEAVY BIT

'The fact, then, that "if any man is in Christ he is a new creation" does not mean that he starts or continues his life in a vacuum, or that his mind is a blank table. It has been formed by his own culture and history and since God has accepted him as he is, his Christian mind will continue to be influenced by what it was before. And this is true for groups as for persons. All churches are culture churches – including our own. But throughout history there has been another force in tension with this indigenizing principle, and this also is equally of the gospel. Not only does God in Christ take people as they are: he takes them in order to transform them into what he wants them to be. Along with the indigenizing principle which makes his faith a place to feel at home, the Christian inherits the pilgrim principle, which whispers to him that he has no abiding city and warns him that to be faithful to Christ will put him out of step with his society; for that society never existed, in East or West, ancient time or modern, which could absorb the word of Christ painlessly into its system.'[3]

In practice, however, missionaries have found that this is even more complicated than it sounds. Take polygamy, for example. Missionaries attempting to disciple new converts understandably took the view that polygamy was unchristian, but made the mistake of insisting that new converts who already had more than one wife get rid of the others. After watching the social havoc this wreaked in villages and the ostracising from society of many of their new converts, some missionaries began to seek another approach. They argued that Christians witness through two basic relationships, church and family, and that culturally appropriate forms of both must be kept as a priority if evangelism is to be taken seriously. This did not mean that polygamy became acceptable, but rather that it was allowed for that generation, hoping that faith would bring about change in the culture over time.[4]

There was the added problem too when it was found that a bad custom could nevertheless have a constructive function within that culture. So, for example, some of the ways that tribes initiated young people to adulthood may well have been cruel and/or immoral, but a clear rite of passage to adulthood was nevertheless important for people. Missionaries found that it was a mistake to stop a custom without at least providing an alternative for the function it provided to the society.[5]

'We did not want the fact that someone was smoking cannabis to be a barrier to him getting to know God. Cannabis was not a salvation issue. If we had told the young people that they could not smoke or drink when they had come into church, then they would not have come at all.'[6]

Here lies the missiological background to the value calls that youth workers are having to make every day in what is acceptable and what needs to be challenged in youth culture.

And it is no less complicated working with teenagers than working with a culture within the developing world. For example, try to divide up the list below into three categories: what always has to stop when some teenagers become Christians; what can be allowed to continue for a time; and what can be affirmed in youth culture.

- Smoking
- Wearing fashionable clothes
- Soft drugs
- Gang membership
- Importance of friends
- Loyally supporting friends in a crisis
- Membership of sports team
- Casual sex
- Sleeping with a regular partner
- Obsessive following of a particular band/singer
- Shoplifting
- Swearing
- Skipping school
- Being rude to parents
- Drinking alcohol under age
- Watching 18-rated videos

> 'The twin dangers in approaching the task of contextualization are the fear of irrelevance if contextualization is not attempted and the fear of compromise and syncretism if it is taken too far.'[7]

Wider application

In 1996 'living in sin' was at last officially dropped from the Church of England's language. Of course, theologically speaking, the phrase was always inappropriate (the whole world lives in sin), but the headline signalled an important process of change as the church rethinks the realities of engaging the modern world. Slowly the church is coming to see that Christian morality is not a barrier that stops people coming to Christ, but rather the maker's instructions for life as he always intended it to be.

As we can see from the table below various models of how the gospel's implications would work out in a given society have been put forward, but at the end of the day the missionaries' lesson for all to hear is that it is only after truly identifying with and appreciating a culture over a sustained period of time that we are able, under God, to make the necessary distinctions required for truly relevant and engaging faith.

A gospel that people can understand

'We will make mistakes in the process of contextualisation, but there is no mistake worse than not trying at all.'[8]

Level	Description	Example
1	Immediately renounced	Idolatry, witchcraft, sorcery, cannibalism, head-hunting, widow-strangling, infanticide, blood feuds, ritual prostitution
2	Tolerated initially, but gradually disappear	Polygamy, caste system, slavery
3	Churches divided on whether level 2 or level 4	Marriage practice and initiation rites
4	Indifferent matters	Eating and bathing customs, ways of greeting the opposite sex, hair and dress styles, music

One of the ideas the missionaries teach us in 'beginning where people are' is to find stories and images in the culture which carry within them elements and values of the gospel. These then act as bridges of understanding for the people whom the missionary is trying to reach. Missionary writers refer to them as 'redemptive analogies'.

Dr Peter Cotterell talks of his work with one of the tribes in Ethiopia, where there is a traditional belief in a god whose name when literally translated means 'the far off god'. He wisely chose this name to explain the incarnation in Amharic and was effectively saying, 'The god who was once far off has now come near.'

In the dramatic book *Bruchko*, Bruce Olson recounts his life among the Motilone tribe of Colombia. After five years of enduring a great deal of suffering he heard of a Motilone legend about a man who became an ant. 'As the story flashed into my mind, for the first time I realised its lesson,' he says. 'If you are big and powerful, you have to become small and weak in order to work with other weak beings. It was a perfect parallel for what God had done in Jesus.' Olson took the word for becoming like an ant and used it for the incarnation. The idea that God became a man 'stunned them'.[9]

Vincent Donovan nearly despaired of his attempts to communicate Jesus to the Masai, because much of the cultural setting of the New Testament itself was entirely alien to the Masai people. Slowly, though, glimmers of light appeared. Donovan discovered, for example, that there were in Masai culture rituals for forgiveness which effectively acted as sacraments to the people. If a son offended his father, it was usually unforgivable, but there was provision among them that spittle could be used as a sign of forgiveness. Spittle was obviously a powerful symbol of life in a dry and parched land, and the father would spit upon the son as a sign of a fresh start for their relationship. Donovan was further encouraged that divided families could be reconciled by the exchanging of food in a special meal. Both of these Masai rituals provided for Donovan the doorways to understanding that he had been searching for.

However, such an approach is obviously fraught with problems. In India, for example, some Christians took the risk of borrowing the word 'avatar' to describe the incarnation of Christ. Despite careful explanations, many Indian Christians refused to use the phrase, as it was originally borrowed from Hinduism and the so-called incarnations of Vishnu. Without great care, redemptive analogies, far from clarifying the gospel message, can actually confuse it.[10]

Don Richardson, in his contemporary missions classic *Peace Child*, describes his frustrations in trying to communicate the gospel to head-hunting Sawi peoples of Papua New Guinea:

> For the Sawi tribe, treachery was the highest virtue, their heroes had all committed great acts of betrayal leading to the slaughter of their 'friends'. To them, Judas was seen as a wonderful hero of treachery. How could they respond to Jesus?
>
> The breakthrough came with an even more powerful story in their own legends of 'the peace child'. Peace could be made by offering one's own child to deadly enemies. God's love in giving his own 'Peace Child' communicated – and many of these cannibalistic peoples have since come to Christ.[11]

Many missiologists believe that God has placed such imagery in every culture.

Redemptive analogies in youth culture

'We allowed some of the imagery and language associated
with drugs to explain ideas about Christianity to the kids.
We were using imagery from Bermondsey to tell young
people about Jesus. This thinking is second nature to African
and Indian theologians, who know that every time you
approach a different tribe you have to learn their customs
before you can speak to them about Jesus. The young people
were like a tribe with their own language and customs and
our job was to root our presentation of Jesus in ideas that
they understood.'[12]

In such a vastly different type of cultural setting, the
redemptive analogies in the world of today's young people
take a very different form. In a culture dominated by the
media, it is inevitably the media, especially through films,
soaps, music and news stories, which provide the bridges
of understanding into which the work of Christ can be
understood today.

Instructor saved Briton in 6,000ft fall
A British skydiver who survived a six-thousand-foot fall
when his parachute failed to open was probably saved by
the sacrifice of the instructor who fell with him.[13]

There are, of course, opportunities other than redemptive analogies which present doorways of understanding
for the gospel in today's culture. While they may not
capture the heart of the gospel message like a redemptive analogy does, they can nevertheless be very valuable
'windows' for understanding. Into this category regularly
come lines from songs in the charts, quotes from media
stars, story lines from the soaps, etc.

This is not to say, of course, that the media provide the

only form of helping the gospel message connect with young people. As we have already seen, the model of Jesus' teaching is very interactive and informal, so family and peer group experiences and the 'hot issues of the moment' for a group of young people are all excellent opportunities.

I once had two very troubled lads in the back of the car as I approached a roundabout. Braking in the normal way, I was hit from behind by another driver who was

FOR ONCE IN THEIR LIVES THE TWO LADS WERE NOW GIVING ME THEIR UNDIVIDED ATTENTION...

simply going too fast. Having checked that the lads were OK, I got out and went to have a word with the offending driver. As I did so, I saw out of the corner of my eye that the two lads had unstrapped their belts, wound down the window and were, for once in their lives, giving me their undivided attention. It struck me that whatever I was to say in the future about handling personal anger, this would be the lesson they would remember. I found the thought a most calming one and the journey home was a once-in-a-lifetime opportunity to really connect with two angry young men about coping with the way they were feeling inside.

A church people can relate to

Once the gospel is being understood, the highest priority for the missionary is to establish a church in which indigenous people feel comfortable; where they can celebrate and learn more about their faith in their own culture. Why? Because worship must be genuine and sincere and this is more likely (though never guaranteed) when church practice is relevant to the culture. Relevance is only a means to an end though, as it is authenticity which is our goal. For this to happen effectively, it is widely recognised that a number of things are important, from the design of the building to the style of dress; from the atmosphere of the meeting to its length; from the style of the teaching to the amount of participation by the congregation and so on.[14]

In his book *Bread of Life*, Ron Sider cites the church in Bali as a leading example of a church truly relevant to its people. Even in 1971, every aspect of the Bali church – its architecture, music and worship – was Western. So much so that Bali Christians were sick of the label 'Black Dutch'. They wanted to end their isolation from Bali culture, so in 1972 Dr Wayan Mastra chaired a watershed synod of Bali Christians. They built a cultural training centre called a temple of meditation that would use Balinese architecture and art to proclaim the gospel in ways relevant to the Bali people 'to help Balinese Christians gain a greater appreciation of their cultural heritage within the context of their faith and to find new ways of expressing that faith within the culture'.[15] The Bali church also recognised that Bali culture is very visual and that words are not enough, so they set about an ambitious programme of social action to demonstrate visually their proclamation of the kingdom of God.

Contemporary church faces the music

Of all the issues related to contextualised church, perhaps the most influential factor that missionaries found in establishing the cultural fit of a church is the style of music used. Here lies a big challenge for today's church.

'The church must celebrate, sing and dance the gospel in its own cultural medium.'[16]

'The solemn silence was then swept away as the assembly hall reverberated with the loud and clear beats of African drums signalling new birth. This was the voice of Christian Africa, not drums calling to the past darkness of pagan rituals, but drums dedicated to God, the transformation of an age-old instrument into an instrument of the church, proclaiming unity and common witness.'[17]

When I started working as a youth minister I was part of a vibrant local church that would best be described as 'renewed evangelical'. At that time, the non-Christian teenagers we were contacting through schools and clubs were interested in church and often enjoyed attending, particularly the evening service. Ten years later, however, despite many improvements in the way the church did things, the evening service was more than many of the Christian teenagers could tolerate, let alone the non-Christians.

Even for teenagers from Christian families, much of what went on was out of tune with their world. To the average member of the congregation, this was incomprehensible. We had moved with the times: we no longer had pews or pulpits, a band had replaced the keyboard, women often led and we even had a video screen and projector. Compared with other churches we were positively trendy. Surely we were more in tune with youth culture now than we ever were? The truth was that we had copied the effect but missed the heart of a changing culture.

A defining moment for me came with the arrival on the wider Christian scene of two young and very gifted worship song writers, Martin Smith and Matt Redman. As Elvis had done in the 1950s for another generation of disenfranchised young people, so Smith and Redman gave a voice to postmodern Christians feeling trapped in a modernist church.

Nowadays with their albums consistently best sellers it seems almost strange to write in this way, but Smith and Redman were the first generation of worship leaders not to have grown up in a hymn culture and their music more naturally reflected a mainstream chart sound. It was impossible to lead this kind of music from a piano or organ, it was a style largely alien to the majority of classically trained musicians and it was loud.

Just as William Booth in the nineteenth century was driven to use the melodies of the music hall to make Christian worship comprehensible for those he worked with in the inner city, so these new writers used styles and images that made Christian worship comprehensible to contemporary youth culture.

Their impact, though, was not just one of style; it was one of substance too. There was a significant shift in the lyrical content of the songs. They dropped much of the well-worn biblical language, familiar both in hymns and modern songs, and allowed the message to become more oblique and at times deliberately vague. They also included a massive injection of hope, anticipation and longing for renewal and revival. Meaning came through pictures more than principle, and above all the music was passionate.

The arrival of this music clearly revealed to me how even renewed evangelicalism was trapped within modernist culture. Introducing the songs into church was fascinating.

For some, here was music that at last gave vent to so much of what they felt in a natural musical form. Here were words that didn't try to box God in and here was music you could really dance to. For the majority of my brothers and sisters in Christ, though, here was a tune they couldn't get, to words they didn't understand, in a style they didn't like.

I began to see that for all the inspiration and variety of Graham Kendrick's work, most churches pick out the ones with a hymn style musically and an objective message lyrically. That is not intended to be in any way critical of Kendrick, who will go down in church history as one of the greatest and most varied hymn writers. It is simply to recognise the day-to-day realities of the local church music.

As youth cultures move on and diversify, of course we must recognise that no one musical style can reach even a majority days and the very notion of Matt Redman and Martin Smith still being cutting edge would bring a smile to the faces of some young people I know.

Nevertheless, in churches up and down the country a question is being posed to the generation of evangelical leaders who emerged in the '80s and early '90s. Did they really push through changes to traditional church music to engage a lost world, or did they do it out of personal preference? It's only their responses to emerging styles of worship that will tell us the answer.

> 'The traditional church are truly God's
> people, but my heart is for the 90 per cent
> of this world who will not traditionalise in
> order to become Christian.'[18]

Perhaps the most famous contemporary church is Willow Creek in the United States. Former staff member Dr. Steve Gerali, professor of youth ministry and adolescent studies at Elgin's Judson College, wrote a powerful challenge on this very issue: 'The contemporary church now sits in the seat of the traditional church and forgets its heritage and the process of contextualisation that shaped its success.'[19]

Still deeper to go

Most worrying of all is what the missionaries were to discover next. After all the struggles of learning to draw the line and not unnecessarily threaten culture; after all the hard work of attempting to contextualise both the gospel and ways of doing church, they found they had to go still deeper. The simple discovery was this: a contextualised gospel message engaged people's minds, and a contextualised church engaged people's emotions, but it took more than that to capture the soul of the people's culture.

> 'If the behavioural scientists are right about
> the nature and extent of the impact of culture
> on people, Christians must face the problem
> squarely.'[20]

Take, for example, Africa. It could be said that a lot of progress has been made in engaging indigenous people with culturally appropriate forms of worship. Proverbs and stories are used in preaching, which encourage oral responses from the congregation. Liturgical dance, based on traditional dances, is used and church music is based on traditional patterns, with active participation by the congregation.

But even here, there is something missing. The key moments of human life – those most important to all of us like birth, marriage, death and burial – are often still marked in two separate ways and in two different places by African Christians. First there is the traditional tribal manner and then there is the 'Christian way', with little interaction or integration between the two – dualism strikes again. In other words, the gospel is not allowed to fully shape the life of the people. The soul of culture still evades the gospel.

This discovery was to have huge implications for the mission movement, many of which it continues to grapple with. Faced with the harsh reality that even after contextualising the gospel message and church methods Christianity was still being tacked on to culture rather than transforming it, the missionary thinkers were forced back to the very core issues of their enterprise. What they were to discover we look at in the next chapter.

'In a sense Christians must begin all over again. Their starting point must be to develop a theology for the African Church that accommodates African culture better than Western theology communicated by missionaries of the past.'[21]

Summary of Chapter 12

Virtually all evangelism today is cross-cultural.

One of youth work's essential contributions to the church is teaching us that we must learn from missionaries if we are to communicate successfully.

In particular we must learn:

- not to inadvertently threaten someone's culture by what we present of the church
- where to draw the line in the engagement between the gospel and a culture
- to communicate a message that people can understand
- a church practice that they can relate to.

Most important of all, though, we must learn that this is still not enough.

Notes

1. Michael Eastman, *Inside Out* (Falcon Books, 1976), p.18
2. Vincent J.Donovan, *Christianity Rediscovered* (SCM Press Ltd, 1978), p.7 of Preface
3. Andrew Walls, *The Missionary Movement in Christian History* (T&T Clarke, 1996) p.7
4. For a fascinating missionary report on this read Walter Trobisch quoted in Paul G. Hiebert, *Anthropolical Insights for Missionaries* (Baker Books, 1985), p.177-179
5. For further insights into the complexity of practical contextualization see Paul G. Hiebert, *Anthropoloigal Insights for Missionaries* (Baker Books, 1985), p.181 f
6. Bob Mayo, *Gospel Exploded* (Triangle Books, 1996), pp.39–40
7. David Hesselgrave and Edward Rommen, *Contextualization* (Baker Books 1989) p.55
8. Priest, *Doing Theology with the Masai* (William Carey Library, 1990), p.208
9. Bruce Olson, *Bruchko* (New Wine Press, 1973), p.141
10. The Willow Bank Report (LCWE, 1978), p.9
11. Don Richardson, *Peace Child* (Regal, 1974)
12. Bob Mayo, *Gospel Exploded* (Triangle Books, 1996), pp.42–43
13. *The Times*, 25 June 1997
14. For an interesting example of this see Paul G. Hiebert, *Anthropological Insights for Missionaries* (Baker Books, 1985), p.32
15. Mackenzie and Mastra, *Mango Tree Church*, p.31, quoted by Ronald Sider in *Bread of Life* (Triangle Books, 1994), p.100
16. The Willow Bank Report (LCWE, 1978)
17. quoted by Hesselgrave and Rommen in *Contextualization* (Baker Books, 1989) p.108
18. Chuck Kraft
19. Steve Gerali, *The Church and Youth Ministry* (Lynx Books, 1995) p.52
20. Documented by Peter Schineller Jnr. in *International Bulletin of Missionary Research*, April 1996
21. Quoted in D Hesselgrave and E Rommen, *Contextualization* (Baker Books, 1992) p.99

13

Missionary Essentials (2)

God does not want us to be instant cross-cultural experts.
He does however want us to begin changing.[1]

Missionary influence

It is worth noting at the start of this chapter that a number
of nationwide initiatives for the wider church over the last
few years have drawn heavily on missionary teaching
and experience.

Missionary Congregations, for example, is a mainly
Anglican movement led by Robert Warren, a former
archbishop's special advisor for evangelism. With the
mottoes of 'reaching more by doing less!' and 'being a
different kind of church', its whole philosophy is very
closely mission linked.

Willow Creek Community Church, which has been
hugely influential in this country over recent years, has
a very carefully focussed mission-based strategy for
the local community. Similarly, Laurence Singlehurst of

YWAM has, in his book *Sowing, Reaping, Keeping,* clearly articulated a mission strategy as foundational for the church in our post-Christian society. It is exciting to see these mission themes being taken up and applied to the local church context.

However, we must be careful. Once again in church history we are in danger of copying the effect and losing the heart of what we are trying to accomplish. As we saw in the last chapter, the missionaries found that contextualising the gospel and ways of doing church was not enough to really capture the heart and soul of people.

Isn't that precisely the situation we find ourselves in today? For all our efforts in reforming our ecclesiology and rethinking our proclamation, as we saw in Chapter 2 Christianity is still caught up in Western culture with a privately engaging but publicly irrelevant faith. Capturing the heart and soul of a people's culture is in no way just an issue for the developing world. It affects you and me.

If our goal is that the whole of life is orientated towards God, if our goal is that the church has no walls to the community, the missionary writers teach us that there is still further to go if we really mean business.

To capture the soul of a culture we first need to go back to the beginning. We need to ask the fundamental questions as the missionaries did about who we are and what we are trying to do.

What is the purpose of mission?

The great missionary writer Roland Allen has been described as a lonely prophet. Writing at the turn of the century based on his experiences in China, his work was always ahead of his time. He argued passionately and strongly that the only way to see a truly at-home and life-engaging expression of Christianity in a culture was for the church to be led from the very start by the people themselves.

> If the first converts are taught to depend upon the missionary, if all work is concentrated in his hands, the community learns to rest passively upon the man from whom they received their first insight into the gospel. Paul founded churches, we found missions.[2]

In his provocative book *Missionary Methods – St Paul's or Ours?*, Allen went against the accepted thinking of his day and challenged the missionary movement to take more seriously the church-planting model of the apostle Paul. The Spirit of Christ is the spirit of initiative. Nothing comes near to Paul when he preached the gospel not the law and then retired from his converts to give place to Christ. To do this, he had the spirit of faith. He was persuaded that the Spirit of Christ would teach them to approve that example and inspire them to follow it. He trusted his converts because he believed in the spirit within them.

> 'Our method has a strong restraining influence. We pray for God to fill converts with zeal and shrink back from the steps which would encourage this.'[3]

The purpose of mission was being redefined. Instead of establishing a church for a group of people, mission was to focus on evangelism and leadership support. The young church could then naturally grow up among the new indigenous converts. Without this responsibility for the future of Christianity in their world, Allen believed that the gospel would never capture the soul of a culture.

The role of the missionary

As the purpose of mission was changing, so the role of the missionary had to change too.

Vincent Donovan was influenced by Allen's work. In his well-known book *Christianity Rediscovered*, Donovan wrote of this process of re-evaluating his missionary role as he tried to discover how to evangelise the formidable Masai tribe.

'It is almost as if the authors of the mission wish upon the third world church all the ills of Western institutionalism. We build a 100 year strategy when what we want to do is not stay longer than necessary. We tend to feel that we need to leave them with an institution before we go. Instead we must leave them with what Paul did. The gospel is the affair of the missionary. Interpretation of the gospel is the affair of the people.

'I would propose cutting myself off from the schools and the hospital and just go and talk to them about God and the Christian message. I have no theory, no plan, no strategy, no gimmicks, no idea of what will come. I feel rather naked. I will begin as soon as possible.'[4]

Donovan set about his task:

'I then pointed out that we were well known among the Masai for our work in schools and hospitals and for our interest in Masai and their cattle. But now I no longer wanted to talk about schools and hospitals, but about God in the life of the Masai and about the message of Christianity. Indeed it was for this very work that I came here from far away.

'Ndangoya looked at me for a long time and then said in a puzzled way, "If that is why you came here, why did you wait so long to tell us about this?"'[5]

'As a missionary in South India, the most basic idea that I had drummed in to me was the idea that no-one should impose an interpretation of Christianity on anybody else, but instead people should be allowed to develop their own understanding of God... Ten years after coming back from India, I was learning to apply the same missionary critique to work in my own country, in Bermondsey.'[6]

Institutionalism

It is worth noting too that pioneering missionaries like Donovan and Allen felt great frustration with the institutional approach of the missionary movement. They found there was no room for direct evangelism and had to ignore the system to conduct it. They were, in effect, highly disruptive. Of course, in doing so they were actually drawing the mission back to its reason for its existence, its true heart.

'I had to plant the seed of the gospel in the Masai culture and let it grow wild.'[7]

Similarly today, young people's work is notorious for not fitting in with the traditional way the church goes about things. Once again we must learn the lessons of the missionary. We must learn that youth workers, far from being disruptive, are actually calling the church back to its true mission. We have to see our structures as a means to an end, not an end in themselves.

> 'Our organisation immobilises our missionaries. It creates and maintains large stations and great institutions and these absorb a very great proportion of our energy. We cannot move freely.'[8]

Participation in mission

We have done everything for them except acknowledge their equality. We have done everything for them, but very little with them. We have done everything for them except give place to them. We have treated them as dear children, but not as brethren.[9]

This change of role for the missionary led to a far greater emphasis on participation by indigenous people in mission activity.

Bishop Lesslie Newbigin writes powerfully of the value of this kind of participation. During his time as a bishop in India he resolutely refused umpteen requests to send missionaries to support young converts in villages throughout his area. Instead he sent trained Indian helpers to advise and support, so that the fledgling church learned right from the start not to be dependent on the mission for its existence. A few years later there was a resurgence of militant Hinduism in the area and all the new churches were approached to renounce their Christian faith. Only one did, and it was the one church to whom a missionary had been sent.

The lesson of the missionaries is that patterns of doing church cannot be imposed upon people of a different culture, but must be entrusted to the Spirit at work in young converts' lives. Worship, leadership and church practice must flow out of the trial and error of the fledgling church interpreting God's word for themselves if that church is to be truly evangelistic and an engaging expression of the Christian gospel to the people of that culture.

These missionaries teach us that leadership is better grown from within than imposed from outside. Not only does this have profound implications for the selection and allocation process of most of the denominations today, but significantly it has a great deal to say about the nature of church leadership in a changing world.[10]

Application for today

Not that we should be uncritical of missionary teaching, of course. First it must be evaluated against the Bible's teaching and then against our own experience. We must also be mindful of a different cultural setting. For all the hardship and loneliness that these missionaries endured, I can't help feeling just a little envious of some of them. After all, they had one defined and stable culture to reach with the gospel. The task of the church in today's Western world is more complicated and involved. Cultural engagement, it seems, involves aiming at a constantly moving target.

For all that, though, there is no doubt in my mind that it is at this point that missionary insights are of perhaps the greatest value to the contemporary church. For all our talk of releasing and equipping the laity, we have actually missed the point.

By the time we release people into church leadership they are already subtly indoctrinated into a church way of doing things. In effect we are not really letting go, merely tinkering with what is already there. The more biblical model rediscovered by the likes of Allen and Donovan is that this delegation of responsibility must start from day

NOW THE STEWARDS WILL WAIT UPON US FOR TONIGHT'S OFFERING...

BY THE TIME WE RELEASE PEOPLE INTO CHURCH LEADERSHIP THEY ARE ALREADY INDOCTRINATED INTO A 'CHURCHY' WAY OF DOING THINGS...

one if the church is ever going to have the fresh cultural cutting edge we all long for, although we must of course hold Paul's model of church planting in tension with his counsel in 1 Timothy 5:22 not to be hasty in setting aside people for leadership.

A great window of opportunity to explore this issue more thoroughly is provided for the church today through its work with young people. It is, however, a window that in some quarters is hung with heavy curtains.

Youth congregations

A youth congregation is not to be confused with a youth church. A youth church is fully autonomous, whereas a youth congregation, while normally meeting separately from the adult church, comes under that church's leadership authority.

There are a growing number of experiments with youth congregations, and their very existence has been more than a little controversial. So what should our response be to youth congregations?

'Perhaps the days of immediately incorporating young people into our existing church structures are over.'[11]

Arguments against youth congregations

Opponents of youth congregations would cite a number of arguments to support their view.

THEY ARE UNBIBLICAL

Authors like Donald McGavron would suggest that church growth in the book of Acts is never limited to a particular group, but includes all people groups. In fact, Gordon Fee is quoted as saying that homogenous (or same people type) congregations have no biblical foundation.[12]

THEY MISREPRESENT THE GOSPEL

Paul makes it so abundantly clear that the nature of church is to model a supernatural oneness to a fragmented world, that to have separate services for young people is a denial of one of the basic gospel principles.

They are illogical

The argument goes that if the church is failing, it is the church that must be changed. It is illogical to set up alternatives.

They short-change teenagers

Most teenagers want to relate to, and be accepted by, adults. If we encourage youth congregations, we take away that opportunity, at least within the church family.

They ignore church history

Michael Harper makes the point (though not about youth congregations *per se*) that when groups separate from organisations out of tension with the old, they subconsciously plan a corrective that successive generations of the movement immediately make normative. In other words, reactions against something always tend to react too far and need to be brought back again.

They are an extension of a failed method

Most youth congregations are really glorified youth groups in disguise. Not a lot has changed in their foundational thinking, merely the trappings and the title. It is still basically a halfway house approach. The teenagers cannot cope with church right now, so the thinking is that we will try to hold on to them for a few years and hopefully they will integrate with the wider church a number of years down the line.

We have to be bold enough to see that this approach has not worked for the last thirty years, so it is hardly likely to get much better in the future, even if we do call it by a new name.

THEY ARE SIMPLISTIC

A youth congregation cannot work, simply because youth culture has separated into so many tribes anyway that what appeals to one will only alienate another, thus perpetuating the problem of failing to truly engage people where they are.

THEY LACK EXPERIENCE AND WISDOM

Pastoral care and counselling are part of normal church life, but if a congregation is going to be made up of only young people, there will be a lack of those with enough life experience and situational stability to support people in need. There is the added problem that with only a few adult leaders around, this can give those leaders an undue influence, which can be unhealthy.

THEY MAKE THE GENERATION GAP WORSE

Far from encouraging unity, youth congregations may only heighten the generational tensions between God's people.

THEY HAVE NO FUTURE

Youth congregations inevitably grow older. Faced with this, what is their long-term purpose?

Take all of the above at face value and it would appear that youth congregations are at best a colossal waste of time and effort, and at worst a strategy straight from hell. By turning to the missionaries, though, the above is put in a different perspective.

First we have to try to understand why the need for youth congregations has arisen in the first place.

'The clear though underlying objective of
much church youth work is to keep adults
happy.'[13]

'Churches want young people like warders
want prisoners – for the roll call.'[14]

Reasons for youth congregations

- A growing number of Christians want to follow Jesus,
  but find church culturally alienating.
- Many young people in the church already feel power-
  less and frustrated by their lack of leadership opportunity.
- A sense of rejection from organised Christianity for
  those who don't quite fit into middle-class society.
- The failure of the church to disciple and pastor young
  people in their own culture.
- To harness the potential of modern media and technology in church communication.
- Youth leaders are becoming exasperated with the established church and want to do something new.

From a missionary perspective

As soon as we start thinking about the issue, a missionary
perspective immediately recognises that evangelism and
discipleship in a person's culture are crucially important
if the gospel's implications are ever to truly impact
society.

What is currently allowed to go on in today's churches
is tragic. Most young people in Britain today never genu-

inely hear the gospel. Those who do, reject it; because they perceive their culture to be threatened by all the trappings of the church. For the tiny minority of young people who do respond to Christ, they are caught between the two worlds of church and culture. A privately engaging but publicly irrelevant faith is often the result.

As we have seen, the only way that the missionaries have found to combat this problem is to allow the converts to shape their own church, to give them the freedom of cultural expression and autonomous leadership. The gospel is the affair of the missionary, the church is the affair of the people.

This is the truly biblical way of dealing with conversion to Christ in a culture different from our own. Fee's point is misleading. It is true that youth congregations (and homogenous congregations in general) have no explicit biblical foundation, but then neither do the sermon and the worship time that are so much part of our church life. It is an argument from silence. The truth is that the book of Acts does not give us a detailed breakdown of the make-up and practice of those early house churches. When one takes on board all the Bible's teaching on culture, to say that youth congregations have no biblical foundation is misleading.

'To the weak I became weak, to win the weak.
I have become all things to all men so that
by all possible means I might save some.'
(1 Cor. 9:22)

The argument that youth congregations ignore the lessons of history is selective at best. We will look at young people in church history in the last chapter, but simply note at this point that evangelical renewal has often gone hand in

hand with the harnessing of new technology. Luther and
the printing press, Booth and the 'music hall approach' for
industrial Britain, even Billy Graham and the evangelistic
rallies (with all the PA and advertising technology they
required) are cases in point. Most youth congregations are
trying to harness new forms of technology to communicate
with the next generation. In doing so, they follow a fine
tradition.

All of the previous objections to youth congregations
cannot be ignored. They have to be addressed if the
congregations are to continue. Ultimately it comes down
to three things: the way the congregation is established,
the relationship it has with the wider church, and the
leadership structure. If the mission writers were to be
heeded properly at these three crucial points, it would
make a tremendous impact. I believe a number of things
would happen.

First, youth congregations would not be called youth
congregations. They would not be trying to reach all
young people or stay forever youthful. The issue is one
of culture, not age. The task is to sow the seed of the
gospel in the non-church culture of new converts and let
it grow beyond that generation and beyond the patterns
of established church (with no expectation that one day
it should come back to look like it either).

Neither would they be a seeker service trying to see
people converted before being grafted in to 'real' church.
It is the responsibility of the new converts to live and act
together as the bride of Christ in their culture.

Congregations would not be set up by frustrated
young people and youth leaders reacting against the
church. Rather they would be encouraged and nurtured
by church leaders themselves as a development of the
church's ministry. Of crucial importance is that the
congregation remain under the pastoral care, teaching

and oversight of the church. Heather Evans makes this point, quoting Priest, a missionary who many years later followed Donovan to work with the Kenyan Masai only to make a sad discovery: 'While Donovan's approach was commendable, in personal visits in the area several years after he left, I was saddened to learn that most all of the new believers had not continued in relation to the church, *due to a lack of continued teaching.*'[15]

This continued teaching is the biblical model. That is the reason for most of the New Testament letters. The churches Paul planted were autonomous and truly indigenous, but they were not simply left on their own to get on with it. They were overseen and supported, challenged and corrected, resourced with both people and teaching. If this relationship were to be recreated today at the local level with so called 'youth' congregations, all the previous objections would be dealt with.

The role of those directly involved in the oversight of a congregation becomes the role of the missionary that writers like Donovan, Newbigin and Allen have defined: encouraging indigenous leadership at every level and allowing the congregation to apply biblical principles in forms culturally appropriate to themselves.

There is no doubt that we are best together, but there is no reason why worshipping in different ways should bring division. With wise oversight the new congregation is free to enjoy a more equal and meaningful sense of unity with brothers and sisters in the adult church, with arranged opportunities to work and pray, fellowship and worship together.

From a missionary perspective, a church that meets in more than one congregation and takes the unique oneness of the body of Christ seriously is both a logical and biblical way forward for the church in the Western world today.

> 'The future agenda for those working with young people it seems will increasingly focus on developing patterns of church life which are able to embrace cultural change and diversity whilst maintaining a gospel commitment to the unity of the church.'[16]

I, for one, have concerns about some current youth congregations, in particular their pastoral oversight and biblical teaching, as well as their long-term strategy. However, it seems clear that rather than standing on the margins, watching and almost waiting for them to fail, every effort should be made to put missionary church planters and youth workers together, lest we miss out on a God-given opportunity for the church in this country truly to engage with our culture, perhaps like never before.

> The movement among young people to express worship in church life within the frameworks of popular culture is both profound and strategic.'[17]

I truly believe that if we would only take the lessons of the missionaries seriously, it would lead to a radical reappraisal of our traditional patterns of church leadership, help us to rediscover a far more robust, practical and participatory missionary model of church, and help us to understand so-called youth congregations not as a threat but more as an opportunity for the church to break free in our contemporary world.

Summary of Chapter 13

Contemporary church is influenced by missionary thinking – but not enough.

When missionary influence goes no deeper than a message people can understand with a way of doing church that they can relate to, the basic problems of the church's culture traps are unlikely to be resolved.

If, however, we learn with the great mission thinkers to re-evaluate our role in mission, the place of the institution in mission and, most of all, the potential of new converts to be God's church in their own culture, then things could be very different.

The essential value of youth work in all this is that the contentious issue of youth congregations requires us to respond to all these issues now.

NOTES

1. Thom Hopler, *A World of Difference* (IVP, 1981), p.192
2. Roland Allen, *Missionary Methods – St Paul's or Ours?* (Robert Scott, 1912). Reset with Memoir Eerdmans Publishing Co., 1962, p.81
3. Ibid.
4. Vincent J. Donovan, *Christianity Rediscovered* (SCM Press, 1978), pp.15–16
5. Ibid., p.22
6. Bob Mayo, *Gospel Exploded* (Triangle Books, 1996), p.9
7. Vincent J. Donovan, Christianity Rediscovered (SCM Press, 1978), pp.15–16
8. Roland Allen, *The Spontaneous Expansion of the Christian Church* (World Dominion Press, 1927, new edition 1962), pp.131–133
9. Roland Allen, *Missionary Methods – St Paul's or Ours?*, p.143
10. To contrast this approach with more usual missionary practice see the approach taken by Anderson and Venn documented in Paul G Hiebert, *Anthropogical Insights for Missionaries* (Baker Books, 1985) p.194-6
11. Laurence Singlehurst quoted in *Alpha Magazine*, Spring 1996
12. Gordon Fee, expounding Romans 8 at the Scripture and Power of God Conference, HTB London, 19 June 1997
13. Peter Ward, *Growing Up Evangelical* (SPCK, 1996)
14. Ibid.
15. Heather Evans, *'Missiological Principles for Youth Ministry'* (dissertation) quoting D. Priest, *Doing Theology with the Masai* (William Carey Library, 1990), p.13
16. Peter Ward, *Growing Up Evangelical* (SPCK, 1996), p.158
17. *Youth Apart* (Church House Publishing, 1996)

14

Leadership Essentials

Church youth work has big implications for Christian leadership, partly because, as we have seen, it tends to act like a trigger for issues crucial to the health and well-being of the whole congregation. In the first part of the chapter we look at some of these.

But perhaps the greatest leadership significance for church youth work is that it has been a powerful formative influence in making the whole church what it is today. If that is the case the great leadership opportunity is that we can, under God, change the future by working with young people now. We look at this in the second part of the chapter.

Part 1

Keeping contemporary

As we saw in Section Two, youthism – the media preoc-cupation with all things young – has a major effect on society. The colossal amount of time, energy, money and resources spent both appealing to and appearing as young, shapes our culture's values, our goals of who we want to be and the lifestyle we want to lead. It is now almost a truism to say that popular culture is youth driven.

What is the importance of this for the church? It is best summed up by American pastor Leith Anderson, author of a number of books on church leadership: 'Those who do not keep up with what is happening with children and adolescents are in danger of being out of touch within twenty-four months.'[1]

Since he penned those words the time has shrunk to more like eighteen months.

It seems the church is always trying to catch up with cultural change. Working closely with young people will help the church keep ahead, not just keep up.

Church growth

Evangelicalism in the United States supports an industry of consultants, advisors, commentators and analysts. For all its excesses, there is little doubt that in its depth and breadth of analysis in church trends, it is without parallel in the world today. For those willing to look, there is a lot to learn from the American church growth movement.

George Barna is one of the leading lights in this industry. Based on his extensive research, he consistently argues that young people's work is crucial to the health of any church. He found that strong, healthy churches placed a high priority on youth work, while weaker ones did not. In his book *Evangelism That Works*, he argues that people go to church not for what they can contribute, but for what they can get. So it is that successful churches are providing 'valuable religious education for children of unchurched parents'.[2]

In his book *User Friendly Churches*, Barna even suggests that ministry to children and young people often has a more profound impact on the spiritual development of their parents than the pastor's teaching does![3] Barna's research also led him to the conclusion that youth work tends to bring a momentum and energy to a church, as well as provide a valuable testing ground for new ideas. He states: 'Ministry to children and youth is difficult in a changing world. It is also absolutely essential for long-term church growth.'[4]

Dynamism

Time and time again, youth work injects energy and momentum into the experience of the adult congregation. Often this is brought about by simple things, like a request for prayer during a youth weekend away, for example. This gives the church a fresh focus, and the encouragement that a youth service brings lifts the mood of a church. Young people taking a summer or a year out to serve God and the commissioning process that goes with it contribute to that often illusive 'feel good factor' in church life. But there are more substantial reasons too for the dynamic youth work brings to a church.

One is creativity. The sheer ingenuity of youth, plus a natural resistance to letting the past dictate the future, means that young people and their leaders often bring a freshness and vitality to church life through creativity. From drama in services to slave auctions for the two-thirds world; from evangelistic escapology to social care sleep-outs; from twenty-four-hour famines to beggars' banquets; from Parable of the Talent weekends to dance and painting in worship – young people with the right encouragement bring a creative energy to church life. One of the sad things, of course, is that we should all thrive on creativity (after all, it is hereditary) but our inbuilt adult reserve sometimes needs the justification that 'it is for the young people' for the rest of us to let our hair down and express ourselves too.

The greatest source of dynamism that youth work brings to the church, though, is conversion. Nothing is more important to Christians than seeing people come to Christ, and statistically most Christians are converted in their teenage years. Ministering to the group with the highest potential of conversion has a way of 'impacting the church environment dynamically'.[5]

Vision

Dynamism and creativity in turn help congregations to begin to map out their future. A sense of momentum brings with it a sense of anticipation for what is around the corner. It is in this atmosphere of hope and expectation that vision begins to emerge.

'A vision catches results in action and a congregation won't move without one.'[6]

Young people can be helpful in this vision-forming process precisely because of what we often think disqualifies them – their youthful idealism. Biblical examples of youngsters like David and Josiah show us that this is often precisely what is needed to offset the sadly too prevalent cynicism and negativism of older Christians. It is often the very fact that young people have not been alive long enough to see some of their dreams crash that makes them of special value in anticipating God's future.

Fewer and fewer youth groups these days are networking in denominational groupings. Church young people today are far more likely to go to interdenominational events like Spring Harvest rather than, say, a Baptist youth convention or Anglican house party. At a very practical level, it makes much more sense for youth leaders to have joint events with youth groups in the same town rather than regional or county events with the same denomination. This all promises much for the future. Instead of being caught up in parochialness, one of the exciting legacies of today's church youth work may be a generation coming through into leadership who think and work more in terms of the kingdom rather than simply the denomination.

'We cannot be the church and cannot confront our culture when our denominations are an inner and spiritual surrender to the ideology of our culture.'[7]

Learning from youthful idealism

It has been noted by a number of educational psychologists that adolescence often includes within it an idealistic phase – a period of thought development in which there is a very strong sense of justice and fairness and in which many views about what is right are shaped without the tempering of broader life experience. In Christian teenagers this can often be reflected in a greater measure of faith.

Many times as I have talked with young people I have found it difficult to keep a straight face, simply because what was being suggested was so totally naive. However, there have been other occasions when I have been profoundly challenged by their simple, trusting faith.

One such occasion was the opening of our Express Bar. The bar was an attempt to create a credible and safe environment for teenagers to spend a Saturday evening. It was to form the successful base of our befriending strategy for a number of years.

Involving the youth group from its conception, we started together to design the layout and decor. At one of those early meetings we chose a two-tier seating arrangement for part of the bar area, and we began what was to become an exhausting search for the stage blocks to make it possible. As we finished in prayer on that first planning evening, one of the teenagers asked God to provide the stage blocks for us. It was a prayer often repeated over the next three months, as everything else (including quadraphonic sound system, a huge array of lighting, video screen and projector, not to mention a twenty-foot bar and the staff to run it) incredibly came together, but not the stage blocks. Nevertheless, despite my cautious noises to the contrary, the team took each new provision we received as confirmation that God was with us and they continued asking in faith for the stage blocks. I had exhausted every possible avenue of enquiry, only to find the prices prohibitive, but three days before we opened, a headmaster in a town twelve miles away rang me and simply said, 'You couldn't use some stage blocks, could you?' They were the ideal size and completely free. All we had to do was go and collect them. It was a huge learning experience for all of us, but I suspect especially for me.

As I reflected on it, Scripture seemed to suggest that adults must be prepared to be humble and learn from this simple uncomplicated faith. 'Young men will see visions,' says the Bible, and David, Josiah and Samuel are all excellent cases in point of a God-given, naive faith which won the day and convinced older and more cynical leaders in the process.

Technology

As steam did to the Industrial Revolution and as the motor car did to the road network, history teaches us that technological development eventually shapes the way we all live. The link between technical innovation and lifestyle is inescapable. It is only a matter of time before one affects the other. We are living through a technological revolution and the implications for the way we all live are as great as were those of the Industrial Revolution for rural Britain in the nineteenth century.

Despite the fact that technology is already changing the way people learn and think, for the vast majority of churches the technological revolution has simply not begun. We may have a computer in the office, but in terms of church teaching, communication and variety in worship the technological revolution still has much to offer. In allowing this to happen, we have forgotten our heritage. The first apostles used the latest technology of the Roman roads to spread the gospel, and our Reformation forefathers were quick to seize on the opportunity that the printing press provided. We must do the same.

Here is another area where young people can help the church. Having grown up in the technological revolution, young people are the most at ease with its implications for the church. Products of a multimedia, interactive world, they expect and demand multimedia communication.

While recognising that high tech is often limited by high cost, we must not simply write it off as too expensive. After all, stained glass windows are expensive. It is a question of priorities. We must also remind ourselves that high-tech must never replace high-touch relational church. Having made both these points, though, if we are truly to engage with our contemporary culture, it is important for the church to address the issue of technology.

There is a place for large video screens with links to computer terminals for graphics and headline texts, as well as DVDs, a proper PA system for our easy listening MP3 culture, slide sequences, live telephone interviews and projected graphic images. With wise use all these can enhance worship in our churches today and make our services more attractive and engaging to a non-Christian society.

I can't be the only youth worker who has spent time and energy fundraising for a large video screen for work with young people, only to find that within a year of purchase the adult church was using it nearly as much as we were. Work with young people encourages the church to make use of modern technology.

Speaking

One of the greatest challenges to those working with young people is also one of the greatest rewards. Public speaking to groups of teenagers is hard work – school assemblies and the like are things that nightmares are made of. They demand brevity, energy, humour, story-telling from an interesting angle, variety of tone and pace and stature, just to keep young people's attention and if you don't hit the mark, they certainly let you know.

However, the benefit of communicating regularly with teenagers is that you become a better speaker. If you can hold their attention, you can hold anybody's and if you can help them understand biblical truth, you can help adults too.

This discipline has left a lasting legacy in the church. Very few of our best preachers and teachers did not learn their trade working with young people. Mind you, it is a discipline that needs to be continued. Working with adult congregations may keep our exegesis sharp, but communication skills can easily get sloppy as adult congregations are just too nice.

PUBLIC SPEAKING TO GROUPS
OF TEENAGERS IS HARD WORK...

Part 2

Back to the future

Just as youth work has shaped the church we have today, so what we do with young people now will shape the church we become in the future.

Pete Ward, a former Archbishop of Canterbury's Special Advisor on Youth Work, has written most extensively on this subject. He argues persuasively that Anglican evangelicalism has been decisively shaped by its work among young people.

Historically, the evidence is persuasive. For example, he shows how the youth work movement CSSM, founded in 1867 (and later to become Scripture Union), was the leading light in helping define evangelical spiritual disciplines such as a daily Bible reading and quiet time and it was they who also first introduced to Christian worship the concept of the chorus. CSSM was a youth movement that, as historian John Pollock has described, 'slowly changed an aspect of British religion'.

Of outstanding influence on the future of evangelical-ism were the CSSM camps started in the 1920s, under the leadership of Eric Nash (known as Bash). 'Bash camps' drew from élite schools and had a massive influence. Converts included John Stott, Michael Green, David Watson and Dick Lucas. Dick Lucas has made it clear that in his mind the training offered by Bash camps was far in advance of anything found in the Church of England's training colleges. By 1982, it is estimated that 7,000 boys had passed through the camps and David Watson wrote that over five years he went to no fewer than thirty-five of them. Alister McGrath has described Bash camps as forming 'a new generation of evangelical thinkers and leaders'[8] and makes particular reference to the importance of John Stott's conversion through the camp, saying that Stott went on to be the most influential evangelical thinker of the post-war period.

Richard Bewdler, himself a graduate of the Bash camps, went on to set up Pathfinders, which has been massively influential in shaping the youth fellowship programme of most Anglican churches. There are few Anglican clergy today who have never attended a Pathfinder or CYFA camp or youth fellowship.

In the early twentieth century came the InterVarsity Fellowship (IVF, later to be called UCCF) to support groups of evangelical students at university. Once again, its impact on evangelicalism has been immense: 'Some of those prominent in leadership of churches, missionary societies and other Christian institutions of many varieties were first spiritually awakened and led to Christ in a university or college Christian Union. They learnt first to take responsibility in active service for Christ when serving on the committee of their student Christian Union.'[9]

IVF was also the birthplace of the Tyndale Fellowship for Biblical Research, which was instrumental in fostering a new generation of evangelical scholars who have in turn shaped evangelical thinking over the period. Another youth work movement, Crusaders, saw among its converts influential figures like Michael Saward and Bishop John Taylor.

Although Ward limits the focus of his research to evangelical Anglicanism, the principle that youth work shapes the future of the church has strong support elsewhere. Clive Calver, who perhaps more than any other individual has shaped much of modern British evangelicalism, started out with British Youth For Christ. Many of Steve Chalke's international media projects were experimented with as a youth minister at Tonbridge Baptist Church, and it was the ministry of Youth For Christ in 1944 that provided the support for a young evangelist who was to go on to become quite influential – Billy Graham.

Adolescent evangelicalism

Not all of youth work's influence has been entirely positive, however. A variety of writers have noted unhelpful characteristics among evangelicals that can be described as adolescent, perhaps as a result of drawing on its youth work roots.

For example, an over-emphasis on simplicity and certainty (so failing to do justice to the mystery and paradox in God's word), an intolerance of those who hold differing views, an authoritarian morality and an unhealthy focus on leadership. All, when analysed, have a genuine 'youthy' feel about them. Is it any wonder, asks Ward, that spirituality which has been so deeply influenced by work among young people is experiencing problems when it seeks to be relevant to older people?[10]

Bash's unintended consequence

As a pioneering and successful model, the Bash camp had its imitators, but once again, as so often in history, the imitators copied the effect and lost the heart of the original. The camps' great strengths can be seen to become evangelicalism's great weaknesses in future generations. Strong Bible teaching and theological correctness in the rarefied atmosphere of camp became a tradition of theologically correct but largely unapplied evangelical teaching.

Many of these early youth work models were also specifically targeted at the privileged classes, with all the cultural trappings of education and money. We are therefore left with methods and patterns of youth work that evolved almost exclusively in the rarefied context of public school and Oxbridge life, and they have not travelled well. 'The history of youth fellowship work in England is therefore largely the story of a movement downwards, the successive leaders attempting to adapt approaches developed in work amongst the upper middle classes to those further down the social scale.'[11]

Protection

Ward also very helpfully reveals the hidden agenda that lies behind much church youth work. He observes that parental concerns often create the environment, both emotionally and financially, for youth workers to be appointed. The unspoken motive is that parents want to keep their teenagers safe. This has some significant consequences. First, one of the chief aims of Christian youth work is to keep Christian teenagers separate from their non-Christian peers and the non-Christian world. Second, this in turn encourages a whole evangelical subculture of alternative music, books, holidays, etc. in which Christian teenagers can be kept safe. The ultimate irony of this protectionist agenda is: 'The chief means for outreach amongst young people which is adopted by evangelical churches is also the means by which those who are not "suitable" are at the same time excluded.'[12]

> We are being to a large extent shaped by our ministry among young people. This means that ministry among young people is one of the key creative places where evangelicalism will renew itself, or not, as the case may be. The future shape of the church is at stake and the church looks to those working with young people for answers.[13]

Even if Ward is only half right (and I for one think that he is a lot more right than that) the strategic significance of the church's work with young people is underlined. If it has got us to where we are, it can lead us to where we want to be.

Revival

Within many quarters of the church there is a renewed interest in, and prayerful anticipation of, revival. Even a cursory glance at revival history reveals the prominent part that children and young people have played in such movements of God's Spirit. Brian Edwards, in his book *Revival*,[14] devotes a whole section to examples of this from around the world. In this country, Harry Sprange has written an exhaustive and thorough work on how Scotland's children have consistently been instrumental in all the periods of revival over three centuries.

'I have just come this morning from an enquiry meeting appointed especially for the children. Several hundreds were present and very many of them were in tears. I could but feel that the Spirit of God was present, convicting of sin. The dear ministers seemed most hearty in their work.'[15]

A very remarkable feature of the movement showed itself in the case of a number of young school boys who started a meeting for prayer amongst themselves. Of such youths as were at this time savingly impressed, not a few subsequently went forth as missionaries to China, India and Africa, while others filled pulpits at home.[16]

Scottish revivals involved children at every level. They saw miraculous healings of young people, witnessed parents converted through their children, saw children going to school to 'fight for Jesus', witnessed children and young people leading prayer meetings alone and saw them publicly giving testimony to their new faith in Christ.

In 1868, in one such period of revival in Scotland, C.H. Spurgeon put his considerable weight behind the specialist children's meetings taking place. His words show great wisdom and insight into what was quite a controversial issue in his day:

'Prayer meetings for boys and girls judiciously conducted will be of abundant service. There should always be an experienced lover of children at their head and then the fewer grown up persons tolerated in the room the better. When there are half a dozen praying children present, their earnest prayers and tears will be with those of their own age, the most potent instrumentality imaginable. Never fear precocity. There is much more danger of indifference and levity. Let wisdom and love preside... We have never developed the capabilities of youth as we should have done.'[17]

Sprange's careful detailed study of Scotland's children and young people in revival deserves serious attention. If children and young people have been prominent in revivals of the past (during a period of history in which young people were far less influential than they are today), how much more strategic will their role be in any revival of the future? Surely it's pure escapism to wait and pray for revival but not do anything to prioritise our work with children and young people now.

The Jesus Movement

One of the reasons we must be ready next time is that we have missed it before.

The Jesus Movement in the 1960s was the hippy generation's response to the traditional Christian church. While it is dangerous to generalise about the movement (as it covered, for example, the breadth of theological conviction from ultra-charismatic to ultra-conservative), members were basically united in a belief that the traditional church had failed to live as Jesus taught. Especially in the United States they ran homes for between six and fifteen members (modelled around the hippy communes) and sought a better world system through living by the book, trusting God and developing a simple lifestyle. Evangelistically, they were by far the most successful Christians of their day in reaching hippies for Christ, partly because they placed great emphasis on treating people with dignity and taking time to answer questions (a reaction against the fundamentalist proclamation preaching of the conservative evangelicals), and partly because they had a characteristic straightforward no-nonsense approach to the message, e.g. boycott hell! One commentator said at the time, 'It could spell the beginning of a great spiritual revolution, comparable to the Reformation.'[18]

However, the irony was that while the Jesus Movement rejected the traditional church, it actually needed the traditional church's input. Its anti-intellectualism, its despising of those who earned money and its general blindness to its own hippy culture's conditioning all required balancing, and the traditional church was the only means of this happening. However, by and large this did not happen because neither the church nor the Jesus Kids could overcome their cultural barriers, and as a result the movement dissipated over time.

While there has been a lasting legacy of the Jesus Movement in this country (including the Good News Bible, Graham Kendrick and Greenbelt Christian Arts Festival), one cannot help thinking about what might have been if only cultural barriers could have been overcome for the sake of Christ.

'If we don't disciple these kids, if the Jesus Movement folds, it will be the church's responsibility. If we just bend, we will see the greatest revival there has ever been, but if this Jesus Movement does not go on, you can put it down to the church blew it.'[19]

Historical cycles

There is one other pointer to the historical significance of youth work which I want to draw attention to.

Dr Mark Senter earned his PhD by researching the history of youth ministry in the United States. As many other historians and sociologists have done before him, he argues that history goes in cycles and that the history of youth ministry is no exception.

In his book *The Coming Revolution in Youth Ministry*, Senter traces cycles in the Sunday school movement of the 1820s, the Christian Endeavour movement of the 1880s and the Youth For Christ movement of the early twentieth century. He concludes: 'A study of history suggests we are about to see a fundamental departure from what we have understood to be youth ministry during the closing decades of the twentieth century.'[20]

He goes on to predict that this coming revolution will be led by youth workers, frustrated by the encumbrances of institutional religion, who break out and try something new. Why is this essential for today's youth leaders to know? Because:

In each of the previous cycles of youth ministry, the sharpest criticism has come from the professional clergy. ... the coming revolution will [again] generate extensive criticism.[21]

If Senter is right, history is in danger of repeating itself. We saw with the Jesus Movement a new move of God, but its enormous potential was lost because the church could not drop its cultural baggage enough to help refine and focus the vision. Youth congregations have a wonderful potential to engage a new generation for the gospel. Let us not make the same mistake again.

Summary of Chapter 14

Young people are an immediate priority for all Christian leaders because of the way they dynamically impact church life with vision, energy and growth.

Young people are a strategic priority for all Christian leaders because of the way youth work powerfully shapes the church of the future.

Young people are now a critical issue for all Christian leaders. The emergence of controversial youth congregations requires that we lay aside our own cultural baggage and come alongside young people in our churches for the sake of the gospel.

Notes

1. Leith Anderson, *Dying for Change* (Kingsway [Nova])
2. George Barna, *Evangelism That Works* (New Wine Regal Books)
3. George Barna, *User Friendly Churches* (New Wine Regal Books), ch.11
4. Ibid.
5. Ibid.
6. Anon.
7. Lesslie Newbigin, *Foolishness to the Greeks* (SPCK, 1985)
8. Alister McGrath quoted by Peter Ward, *Growing Up Evangelical* (SPCK, 1996), p.6
9. Douglas Johnson, *Contending for the Faith*, p.301, quoted by Pete Ward, op. cit., p.33
10. Pete Ward, op. cit., p.43
11. Ibid., p.45
12. Ibid., p.185
13. Ibid., p.216
14. Brian H. Edwards, *Revival* (Evangelical Press, 1990)
15. *Word & Work*, 19 December 1862, quoted by Harry Sprange, *Kingdom Kids* (Christian Focus Publishing, 1994), p.108
16. John Horn, *Reminiscences* pp.48–49 quoted by Harry Sprange, op. cit., p.167
17. C.H. Spurgeon, *The Sword and the Trowel* (London, 1868), pp.149–150 quoted by Harry Sprange op. cit.
18. Roger C. Palms, *The Jesus Kids* (SCM Press, 1971).
19. Richard Hogue quoted by Roger C. Palms, *The Jesus Kids* (SCM Press, 1971)
20. Mark Senter III, *The Coming Revolution in Youth Ministry* (Victor Books, 1992), p.15
21. Ibid., p.181

Conclusion

So what will it take to see this partnership between the church and young people?

The apostle Peter was not known for his humility – far from it – and for a strong, dogmatic man like him, following Jesus had been a hard, breaking journey. His cowardice and betrayal had been very public, of course, but there were also the subsequent struggles and conflicts as God slowly rid him of all his Jewish prejudice and the full implications of the gospel only slowly dawned on him.

But by the time Peter neared the end of his life, he had learned his lesson: 'To the elders among you ... Be shepherds of God's flock that is under your care, serving as overseers ... Young men, in the same way be submissive to those who are older. *All of you, clothe yourselves with humility towards one another, because, "God opposes the proud but gives grace to the humble."'* (1 Pet. 5:1–5, my italics.)

In these verses lies the key to safeguarding the essential role that young people can play in the church. It is very simple, it is the way of Christ, it is one word: humility.

It is the word to which the missionaries have returned time and time again. When the Lausanne Congress published their report on reaching people of different cultural groups, they made the following points about the need for humility.[1]

All Christians need:

- the humility to recognise that we are all prisoners of our own culture
- the humility to understand and appreciate the culture to which we go
- the humility to begin where people are, not where we would like them to be
- the humility to recognise that the best of us will not communicate as well as a trained local indigenous person
- the humility to trust the Holy Spirit, without whom our witness is futile
- the humility to follow Christ in renouncing and sacrificing the things of our background
- in humility to identify with people of a different background.

It is therefore fitting that this book should end with a call to the church for humility towards young people made by one of the greatest missionaries of the modern age. The last word goes to Lesslie Newbigin.[2]

I have often heard people say that youth work is very important because the young people of today are the leaders of tomorrow. But this is surely the wrong way to look at the matter. We have to be concerned about young people not because they will be old later on, but because they are young now!

What really is at issue in this tension between age and youth? Is it not this, that the experience of us who are old, the experience which we think is our greatest asset in comparison with the young is a sinful experience, an experience full of compromise with the world, the flesh and the devil? The point is that we must have young people in the church because we must listen to them, because they have something to say to us, because they put radical questions to us about the way we have conformed to this world.

The tension between young and old in the church can be a fruitful tension if we follow the advice of St Peter and clothe ourselves – young and old alike – with humility, so that we can really listen to each other. Only a church which does that will find the secret of constant renewal.

NOTES

1. The Willow Bank Report (LCWE, 1978), pp.16–17
2. I have taken the liberty of re-arranging the text, though not the meaning, of Newbigin's writing in Lesslie Newbigin, *The Good Shepherd* (The Faith Press, 1977), pp.83–84

Youthwork – the Partnership

Oasis, the Salvation Army, Spring Harvest, Youth for Christ and Youthwork Magazine are working together to equip and resource the church for effective youth work and ministry.

Youthwork – the Initiatives

1. *Youthwork – the Conference*
- An annual training conference to inspire, network and equip – managed by Spring Harvest.
www.youthworkconference.co.uk

2. *Youthwork – the Magazine*
- A monthly magazine providing ideas, resources and guidance – managed by CCP.
www.youthwork.co.uk

3. *Youthwork – the Training*
a) What Every Volunteer Youth Worker Should Know
- A nine-session/18-hour foundation course for volunteer youth workers – managed by Oasis Youth Action, with support from the Salvation Army.
www.oasistrust.org/youthworkcourse

b) The Art of Connecting
- An eight-session/12-hour course for young people in 'three story' evangelism – managed by YfC.
www.yfc.co.uk

4. *Youthwork – the Website*

- A gateway to online resources, community, information and learning – managed by *Youthwork Magazine*.
  www.youthwork.co.uk

5. *Youthwork – the Resources*

- A range of books and materials edited by Danny Brierley and John Buckeridge – managed by Spring Harvest Publishing, an imprint of Authentic Media.
  - Going Deeper – theory, theology and practice.
  - Developing Practice – 'how to' guides, methods and inspiration.
  - Resourcing Ministry – ready-to-use ideas.

Youthwork – the Partners

Oasis Youth Action

Oasis Youth Action, the youth division of Oasis Trust, empowers young people and equips youth workers.

Oasis Youth Participation empowers those aged 11 to 25 years
- *Passion* mobilises young people in social action.
- *Frontline Teams* is a UK-based gap year programme.
- *Global Action Teams* place young adults in different countries.

Oasis Youth Work Training equips youth workers and ministers
- *What Every Volunteer Youth Worker Should Know* is a 9 session/ 18 hour course for volunteers.
- *Youth Work Degree* (BA Hons/ DipHE) is a professional training programme in youth work and ministry.

Oasis Youth Esteem enables youth workers and church volunteers to support young people's personal, social and health education in their local schools.

Oasis Youth Inclusion tackles social exclusion among young people and children. It offers mentoring, group work and sexual health/relationship education.

To find out more about Oasis Youth Action:
Visit: www.oasistrust.org/youthaction
Email: youthaction@oasistrust.org
Phone: (+44) 020 7450 9044.
Write to: Oasis Youth Action, 115 Southwark Bridge Road, London, SE1 0AX, England.

Salvation Army Youth Ministry Unit

The Youth Ministry Unit exists to resource and develop youth work in 1000 Salvation Army centres around the UK and the Republic of Ireland. It works with the Salvation Army's 18 divisional headquarters to implement local strategies for corps/churches, church plants, youth congregations, social centres and youth inclusion projects. In creating leadership development and mission training programmes for young people, young adults and youth workers, the unit is constantly engaged in developing leaders and missionaries for a 21st century church. In pioneering new projects and programmes, the unit is committed to developing new models of mission. In prioritising the marginalised and the excluded, the unit aims to extend The Salvation Army's rich heritage of social action and social justice. It provides young people with regular opportunities to experience, and engage in, evangelism, worship, discipleship and social action within youth culture. At present the unit is developing a new sub-brand of The Salvation Army focused on young people and young adults. In all this the unit aims to equip, empower and enable young people to reinvent The Salvation Army in their own community, context and culture.

To find out more about the Salvation Army Youth Ministry Unit:

Visit: www.salvationarmy.org.uk
Email: youth@salvationarmy.org.uk
Phone: (+44) 020 8288 1202
Write to: Salvation Army Youth Ministry Unit, 21 Crown Lane, Morden, Surrey, SM4 5BY, England.

Spring Harvest

Spring Harvest is an inter-denominational Christian organisation whose vision is to "equip the Church for action". Through a range of events, conferences, courses and resources they seek to enable Christians to impact their local communities and the wider world. Spring Harvest Holidays provide an opportunity in France for relaxation and refreshment of body, mind and spirit.

Their Main Event, held every Easter, attracts some 60,000 Christians of all ages, of which over 10,000 are young people. This event also includes specific streams which cater for over 2000 students. Alongside the teaching programme, Spring Harvest provide a range of resources for young people and those that work in youth ministry.

To find out more about Spring Harvest:
Visit: www.springharvest.org
Email: info@springharvest.org
Phone: (+44) 01825 769000
Write to: Spring Harvest, 14 Horsted Square, Uckfield, East Sussex, TN22 1QG, England.

YfC

YfC, one of the most dynamic Christian organisations, are taking good news relevantly to every young person in Britain. They help tackle the big issues facing young people today. They're going out on the streets, into schools and communities and have changed the lives of countless people throughout the UK.

Their staff, trainees and volunteers currently reach over 50,000 young people each week and have over 50 centres in locations throughout the UK. They also provide creative arts and sports mission teams, a network of registered groups and a strong emphasis on '3 story' evangelism. YfC International works in 120 nations.

To find out more about YfC:
Visit: www.yfc.co.uk
Email: yfc@yfc.co.uk
Phone: (+44) 0121 550 8055
Write to: YFC, PO Box 5254, Halesowen, West Midlands B63 3DG, England.

Youthwork Magazine

Youthwork Magazine is published monthly by CCP Limited. It is Britain's most-widely read magazine resource for equipping and informing Christian youth workers. It provides ideas, resources and guidance for youth ministry. CCP also publish *Christianity+Renewal, Christian Marketplace* and *Enough* magazines. CCP is part of the Premier Media Group.

To find out more about Youthwork Magazine:
Visit: www.youthwork.co.uk
Email: youthwork@premier.org.uk
Phone: (+44) 01892 652364
Write to: Youthwork Magazine, CCP Limited,
            Broadway House, The Broadway,
            Crowborough, TN6 1HQ, England.